TWAYNE'S WORLD AUTHORS SERIES

A Survey of the World's Literature

MEXICO

Luis Davila, Indiana University

EDITOR

Emilio Carballido

TWAS 561

Emilio Carballido

EMILIO CARBALLIDO

By MARGARET SAYERS PEDEN

University of Missouri, Columbia

TWAYNE PUBLISHERS

A DIVISION OF G. K. HALL & CO., BOSTON

Copyright © 1980 by G. K. Hall & Co.

Published in 1980 by Twayne Publishers,
A Division of G. K. Hall & Co.
All Rights Reserved

Printed on permanent/durable acid-free paper and bound
in the United States of America

First Printing

Library of Congress Cataloging in Publication Data

Peden, Margaret Sayers.
Emilio Carballido.

(Twayne's world authors series ; TWAS 561 : Mexico)
Bibliography: pp. 183–89
Includes index.
1. Carballido, Emilio—Criticism and interpretation.
PQ7297.C2482Z8   862   70–1033
ISBN 0–8057–6403–8

For Bill

Contents

About the Author

The author is Professor of Spanish at the University of Missouri, Columbia, where she received her Ph.D. degree in Romance Languages in 1966. She is the author of many articles on Spanish American theater and contemporary Spanish American literature, and has translated works of Carballido, as well as Jorge Díaz, Egon Wolff, Horacio Quiroga, Octavio Paz, Carlos Fuentes, and Pablo Neruda. She serves on the editorial board of *Latin American Theatre Review, Translation Review,* and the Candilejo series of the *American Hispanist.* She is former chairman of the Department of Romance Languages at her University.

Preface

Emilio Carballido is Mexico's premier dramatist. Playwright, teacher, and director of several schools of drama, Carballido has influenced contemporary Mexican theater more than any modern playwright. And in 1975 Carballido celebrated twenty-five years of unequaled theatrical activity.

Carballido is not solely a dramatist. To overlook his four novels and collection of short stories would be a disservice to the literature and to the author. His narrative prose is an important contribution, and minor reputations have been founded on less. Nevertheless, when one says "Carballido," he inevitably evokes the image of theater: some thirty-three brief plays, sixteen full-length plays, spectacles, recreations, ballets, and uncounted movie scripts—these are the amazing accomplishments of Emilio Carballido.

This study is primarily a presentation of the works of Emilio Carballido. I hope it may be an aid to students, a tool for individual investigation into the man's work, and, it is to be hoped, an introduction to those who may not have been acquainted with a rich and varied body of literature.

To accomplish this goal, I have divided Carballido's work into chapters dictated by what seems to be natural divisions in his work. I begin with his brief plays; this was the first genre Carballido attempted; his career begins with the one-act play. From brief plays I move to brief narrative prose, the short stories collected in *La caja vacia*. His four novels follow, in chronological order. Then the full-length plays, which are divided into categories designated as "conventional" and "nonconventional." Where logic permits, the works are considered in chronological order. Where a more insistent pattern imposes itself, I have yielded to logical classifications based on style and theme. The last two chapters are devoted to an overall discussion of Carballido's work.

Although my primary purpose is to present a thorough overview of Carballido's writing to date, I have not included some items in this study. The movie scripts, for example, are not easily obtained, and Carballido himself has said that they are not his proudest accomplishment. Though this may reflect a personal prejudice, and may, in fact, ultimately prove to be a shortcoming, I have not included children's theater, and a number of "spectaculars" conceived by Carballido.

Again, a point that reflects a personal idiosyncracy: as I dislike the disruptive rhythms and effects caused by "language hopping," I have translated all passages from Carballido's work into English. The sources are clearly indicated, and the student who wishes to consult the original will have no difficulty in locating it.

Any student of theater (indeed, of any Latin American genre) can testify that the primary difficulty in this area of research is simply that of *obtaining* the works. Plays are often published (and perhaps never performed) in journals that have but a brief life. Plays may be performed, but never published. Documentation in the form of articles, reviews, notices of performance may be gathered after many hours of research in scattered journals and periodicals, and then often prove to be inaccurate. One thing is clear: Latin American theater awaits its bibliographers! I raise this point merely to emphasize that my efforts in this area have been made infinitely lighter by the always amiable and enthusiastic cooperation of Emilio Carballido. I hope that my obvious interest in his work may in some way repay this most pleasant association through the years. (As this manuscript goes to press, Carballido has written a number of brief plays and one full-length play, *Fotografía en la playa*, which cannot, because of problems of time, be included. Every work on Carballido will, necessarily, be incomplete until such time as he ceases to be a "living author.")

MARGARET SAYERS PEDEN

University of Missouri, Columbia

Acknowledgments

The University of Missouri, and the Department of Romance Languages, have been generous with me over the years, granting me a number of leaves and, through the Research Council, assisting me with typing and research. I would like to take this opportunity to express my gratitude. I am tremendously indebted to Emilio Carballido for providing me with manuscripts and information.

And especially, and above all, I am grateful to my husband, for his support and encouragement.

Chronology

1925 May 22, Emilio Carballido born in Córdoba, Veracruz, to Francisco Carballido and Blanca Rosa Fentanes. At the age of one he is taken to Mexico City where he lives until 1939.

1939 Key year, joins father in Córdoba; experiences change from city life to life in a provincial town. First experience with the jungle and the sea.

1940 Returns to Mexico City.

1946 Writes first play, *Los dos mundos de Alberta.*

1948 First published work, "La zona intermedia." First performed works, "El triángulo sutil" and "La triple porfía."

1950 Like 1939, a turning point. Birth of only son. First commercial productions, "La zona intermedia" and "Escribir, por ejemplo...," open same day at different theaters. *Rosalba y los Llaveros* inaugurates International Season of INBA. Trip to New York on Rockefeller fellowship.

1953 Unsuccessful production of *La sinfonía doméstica* which leads to period of depression.

1954 Year of recovery. Assistant Director of School of Theater at Xalapa. Writes prolifically: *La hebra de oro, Felicidad, La danza que sueña la tortuga, La veleta oxidada,* short stories.

1955 Wins several prizes, "El Nacional," INBA, and UNAM. *La danza*... premiered under title *Palabras cruzadas.*

1956 First novel, *La veleta oxidada.* First performance of *La hebra de oro* in Auditorio Reforma.

1957 Long trip through Europe and Asia as public relations advisor for the National Ballet. First performance of *Felicidad* (Juan Ruíz de Alarcón prize). Publication of *La hebra de oro* and *D.F.*

1959 Second novel, *El norte.*

1960 *El teatro de Emilio Carballido. Las estatuas de marfil* published, also performed in Teatro Basurto. "Homenage a Hidalgo" in Bellas Artes.

1961 "Die Parisiten" ("Las parásitas") in *Spiele in einen akt*, Frankfurt. Menorah de Oro for screenplay "Macario."

1962 Second edition of *D.F. La caja vacía* (short stories). Casa de las Américas prize for "Un pequeño día de ira." "Teseo." "Der friede nach dem dampf" ("La paz después del combate") in Germany.

1963 First trip to Cuba; member Casa de las Américas jury.

1964 Second and third trips to Cuba. *Silencio, pollos pelones* . . . published; performed in Teatro Urueta.

1965 Third novel, *Las visitaciones del diablo*. Television performance of *El relojero de Córdoba* in Havana. Visiting professor, Rutgers.

1966 *Medusa* at Cornell. "Yo también hablo de la rosa" in Teatro Jiménez Rueda (Juan Ruíz de Alarcón and *Heraldo* prizes). "I fiore bianchi" ("Las flores blancas") anthologized in Milan. Travels to Germany at invitation of their State Department.

1967 *Te juro, Juana* . . . at Teatro el Granero (*Heraldo* prize). "Un pequeño día de ira" televised in Havana. *El norte* in *Dos novelas mexicanas*, Montevideo.

1968 Traveling in Spain. *Medusa* in Cultural Olympics accompanying international games. *El norte* in English. *Silencio, pollos pelones* . . . at Scripps College and the Patricio Lumumba University in Moscow. *Acapulco, los lunes* published.

1970 Visiting professor, University of Pittsburgh. Fourth novel, *El sol*. Premiere of *Un vals sin fin sobre el planeta*. "La desterrada" in *El cuento mexicano*, Spain.

1971 Participates in International Theater Festival in Calí. English translations of *El día que se soltaron los leones*, "Yo también hablo de la rosa," and collected plays.

1972 Text edition of *Medusa*. *Felicidad* and "A Short Day's Anger" published. "Teseo" in Norwegian on Norks Rikskringkasting, Oslo. Third edition of *D.F.* French premiere of "Et moi aussi, je parle de la rose."

1974 *El relojero de Córdoba* in Prague.

1975 Adaptation of Cervantes' *Numancia* in Guanajuato. "La

paz después del combate" anthologized in Poland. Director of cultural programs at the University of Veracruz.

1976 Performances of "Un pequeño día de ira," "Homenaje a Hidalgo," "Un cuento de Navidad," *Te juro, Juana* . . . , and *Rosalba*. New editions of *Teatro de Emilio Carballido* and *La caja vacía*. Invited to Venezuela by the Consejo Nacional de Cultura.

1977 February, Sociedad de críticos y cronistas Award for best work of year for "Un pequeño día de ira." New edition of *D.F.*

CHAPTER 1

Carballido and His Time

I Carballido and Contemporary Theater

BY the coincidence of his birth in 1927 and, subsequently, of his first published work in 1948, Emilio Carballido belongs to the single period of greatest renovation and achievement in Mexican literature, the years following the end of World War II.[1] But this coincidence is appropriate, since Carballido has made a major contribution to the phenomenon, particularly in theater.

Even before the discovery of the continent by Western civilization there was theater in Spanish America. It is believed that there was a large body of pre-Colombian plays, largely in the oral tradition, and the authenticity of the *Rabinal Achí* of the Maya-Quiché has been well established. Various theories have been advanced to explain why so few plays actually survived, perhaps one of the most convincing, the desire of the Indians to guard their religious secrets from their conquerors. But even without the physical evidence of manuscripts or copies it is clear that the tradition of theater existed, and in his third letter to the Spanish king, Cortes himself described a "stone masonry theater" in Tenochtitlán.

The Spanish soldier-priests were quick to realize the advantages of this natural receptivity to drama, and in a very short time, probably as early as 1526, the missionaries were employing theater to instruct the indigenous populations and to promulgate the teachings of the church. These religious "lessons" were played in pantomime, in the native tongues, and, later, in Spanish. Soon, too, Western secular theater was introduced to the new continent in the form of plays presented on occasions of state visits or in celebration of holidays or viceregal birthdays, and while the didactic theater of the priests

17

began to decline by the end of the sixteenth century, the courtly theater intended for the Spanish colonists remained in full sway. It should be noted that of all literary genres, theater flourished most rapidly in the New World. Lima and Mexico City were centers for theater before the Pilgrims had arrived at Plymouth Rock, and in the first century following the conquest the importation of Spanish actors, or *authors*, as they were called, was a commonplace in the principal centers of population.

Through the four centuries of Mexican theater one even notes an occasional flash of genius. Sor Juana Inés de la Cruz, or Juana de Asbaje, the brilliant seventeenth-century baroque poet and dramatist, a principal influence in Carballido's work, is the most notable example. In general, however, theater in Mexico, and throughout Latin America, was deeply indebted to the models of its Spanish heritage, whatever the level of its excellence. It is precisely in the present century that one may point to the stirrings of an original body of plays that are specifically Mexican. As Frank Dauster noted in his history of Spanish American theater, "Unlike the Rio Plate theater, which enjoyed great activity, and which found itself upon the threshold of a decade of great enterprise, the Mexican theater at the beginning of the twentieth century lay in a state of almost total decadence."

The renovation of modern Mexican theater begins in the 1920s with the activities of the Union of Seven Authors who because of their intense interest in experimental writers outside of Mexico were called the "Pirandellos." The group, whose most influential member was Francisco Monterde, was devoted to the goal of creating a Mexican—as opposed to Spanish New World—theater. The need for the distinction may be seen in the fact that as late as the first quarter of this century the influence of Spanish theater, Spanish plays, Spanish directors and actors was so strong that Mexican actors performing on a Mexican stage spoke with the distinctive Castilian accent of Spain. The individual successes of the members of the Union of Seven never fully achieved their goals, nor were they as experimental in their plays as in the ideals outlined in their manifesto exhorting the models of European and North American dramatists like Strindberg and O'Neill. But Monterde's *Proteo* (1931) had the distinction of being the first play by a Mexican playwright to be performed by a group dedicated to experimentation.

Later in the same decade a second and more successful group of experimentalists emerged, and in 1928 Xavier Villaurrutia and Celestino Gorostiza, standard-bearers of the literary group of the same name, founded the Ulysses Theater (Teatro Ulises). The members of this amateur group, continuing the interests of the Union of Seven and reacting against the extreme nationalism of many art forms of the years following the Mexican Revolution, again turned outside Mexico toward Europe and the United States for inspiration, translating and emulating authors of a more sophisticated theatrical tradition. Though the life of their theater was of short duration, the spirit of the Ulysses group was continued in Celestino Gorostiza's Orientation Theater (Teatro Orientación, 1932–34, 1938–39) and the Scholars' Theater (Escolares del teatro) founded by Julio Bracho in 1931.

The 1940s witnessed a second surge of experimentation, and again small theaters were formed with the purpose of staging plays that stood little chance of success in commercial theaters. An important factor in this decade was the support given to experimental theater by the government when in 1947 the prestigious National Institute of the Arts (Instituto Nacional de las Bellas Artes, or INBA) established a Department of Theater and a School of Dramatic Art and initiated a series of yearly theater festivals. Equally important during the forties was the continuing influence of the theater of the National University under the direction of Fernando Wagner.

This was the favorable climate awaiting the publication and staging of Carballido's first plays. It would be ridiculous to imply that Carballido was single-handedly responsible for the phenomenon of a new theater in Mexico. On the other hand, contemporary Mexican theater without his presence would be perceptibly less exciting.

If one considers the four principal dramatists who precede Carballido, his contribution to Mexican theater becomes apparent. Of the four, two were avowed experimentalists, Gorostiza and Villaurrutia; the other two were Salvador Novo and Rodolfo Usigli. It is significant that each of these four (the youngest of

whom was born in 1905) continued to write after the beginning
of Carballido's career, so that his predecessors become his contemporaries. What is perhaps more interesting is that the best-
known plays of the four—in spite of the history of their commitment to experimentation—still are predominantly realistic
and regrettably lacking in universality. For example, Gorostiza's
El color de nuestra piel (1952), one of the first serious investiga-
tions of racism in a supposedly racially integrated nation, is more
to be commended for its social criticism than for dramatic excellence. Villaurrutia's *Invitación a la muerte* (1947) is a better
play than *El color de nuestra piel,* but in spite of the vaguely
mysterious overtones, it too is marred. Set in a funeral parlor,
revealing cautious approaches toward innovative techniques, it
might in some ways be considered a forerunner to recent interest in macabre social conventions concerning death. More likely,
it reflects Villaurrutia's well-known personal obsession with
death—an obsession, incidentally, observed in much of Mexican
art and literature. Villaurrutia's real contribution to Mexican
theater lies in his one-act plays which are substantially more
adept and innovative, and, unfortunately, much less widely
studied.

The third dramatist of this same general period, Salvador
Novo, as a collaborator in the Ulysses group of the 1920s, would
also seem to belong to an earlier generation. But Novo's most
familiar plays were published in the 1950s, studies of social
hypocrisy that in the following decade led to less socially
oriented and more adventurous plays based on Aztec and Greek
myth.

The most important of the four dramatists who both precede
and coexist with Carballido is undoubtedly Rodolfo Usigli. Independent of any group, probably more influenced by English
and Scandinavian playwrights than other Spanish American
writers of the time, Usigli has written prolifically. His *El gesticulador* (first staged in 1947) is a landmark in Spanish American
theater. At times agonizingly realistic, it may be most interesting
as an antecedent to Octavio Paz's famous character study of the
Mexican personality, *El laberinto de la soledad.* Perhaps Usigli's
most significant artistic contribution to the genre is his Crown
trilogy. *Corona de sombra,* staged in 1947, is the best of the three

pieces, a light-and-shadow study of the events of the French intervention in Mexican sovereignty and of the light-and-shadow world of its protagonists Maximilian and Carlotta. *Corona de fuego* (1961), whose hero is Cuauhtemoc, and *Corona de luz* (1967), an interesting dramatization of the myths surrounding the origins of the Guadalupe, Mexico's own Dark Virgin, complete the trilogy. In addition to numerous plays best characterized as psychological, Usigli has contributed greatly to Mexican theater as an historian.

Reviewing the best-known plays of these principal figures, it is not difficult to assess what Carballido has contributed to Mexican dramaturgy. While many critics continue to emphasize the importance of his realistic provincial plays, it is more convincing that his real contribution has been the introduction of a vein of fantasy and humor into the realistic tradition, a very personal blend that creates plays that transcend the specifically realistic and restrictively Mexican to achieve a theater that can be called modern, contemporary, and universal, while never losing the specificity of its Mexican origin.

None of the work of these four figures seems greatly to have influenced Carballido's style, although as teachers and mentors of the young playwright, they certainly contributed to his career. Of his true contemporaries, three are especially worthy of mention: Luisa Josefina Hernández, whom Carballido considers to be Mexico's finest dramatist; Sergio Magaña, whose plays show most relationship with his provincial comedies; and Vicente Leñero, a novelist-turned-dramatist whose work to date seems influenced by contemporary documentary theater.

II *Carballido and Contemporary Prose Fiction*

Though Carballido has not had as great an impact on prose fiction as on drama, he has brought an original and distinctive voice to the Mexican novel and short story. And again, as in theater, by accident of timing he belongs to the period of greatest innovation and achievement in prose fiction.

The development of the novel in Mexico to a large degree parallels its development throughout Latin America. Mexico is particularly significant in that development, however, since

the first New World narratives, Hernán Cortes's *Cartas de rela-
ción*, were descriptions of Mexican territories and Mexican
peoples. Cortes's reports to the king were not fiction as such,
but they must have had a similar effect in the Old World considering the "fictional" qualities of the continent he described.
The novel came late to the New World. Although a number
of works, such as the chronicles that described the events of the
conquest and colonization, may be said to have characteristics
of fiction, there is a general critical consensus that the first novel
intended to be read *as* a novel was *El perriquillo sarniento*
(1816). Written by José Joaquín Fernández de Lizardi, this
work again underscores Mexico's general prominence in the
early development of the genre.

The most important historical event of the present century in
Mexico, the Revolution, predictably resulted in a cycle of Revolutionary novels, including some truly noteworthy works like
Los de abajo (1915) by Mariano Azuela and *El águila y la
serpiente* (1924) by Martín Luís Guzmán. The 1930s were
characterized by the novels and short stories of the experimental
group called the Contemporaries (already mentioned in con-
nection with the experimental theater of the same period) which,
in addition to Novo and Villaurrutia, included Gilberto Owen
and Jaime Torres Bodet. However, in the same decade, these
aesthetically oriented novels contrasted strikingly to works of
social realism whose principal practitioners were authors like
Mauricio Magdaleno, José Rubén Romero, and José Revueltas.
It is also in the thirties that the first novel of Augustín Yáñez
was published. It is with Yáñez that the contemporary Mexican
novel comes of age, and, specifically, in the 1940s, with the
publication of his novel *Al filo del agua* (1947). This novel
predates by some ten years the publication of the first of
Carballido's novels. As in the theater, the climate was again
propitious for experimentation.

Among Carballido's contemporaries the novels of Sergio
Galindo are nearest in tone to his own, an observation borne out
by the fact that Galindo's *Polvos de arroz*, and Carballido's
second novel, *El norte*, both published in 1958, were later published jointly in a volume that produces a quiet, but powerful,
portrait of the lives of lonely women who are specifically Mexi-

can, but also sadly universal. Mexico's two internationally known novelists, Juan Rulfo and Carlos Fuentes, seem not to have influenced Carballido, and writers of a slightly younger generation, like Gustavo Sainz, seem more concerned with the techniques of the new novel than with the nostalgic-poetic examination of provincial life that typifies Carballido's five prose publications.

III   *Emilio Carballido*

Emilio Carballido was born in Córdoba, Veracruz, in 1925, the son of Francisco Carballido, a railroad man born in Ejutla, Oaxaca, and Blanca Rosa Fentanes, a native of Cosamaloapan, Veracruz. At the age of one he was taken to Mexico City by his mother where he lived until he was fourteen. This early relationship with his mother had a vital influence on Carballido that continued until her death in 1977.

In 1939 Carballido lived for one year with his father in Córdoba, an experience readily observed in his writing. Carballido has commented on the importance of this move from the city to life in Córdoba in "a big house with a patio and trees and a goat." "It was a world," he adds, "peopled with ghosts and phantoms." At times during that year he traveled with his father, living in railroad cars. This was his first experience with freedom; these were his first trips to the jungle and the sea. It should be noted that the excitement of travel continues to be of paramount importance to this insatiably curious writer. In 1940 Carballido returned to Mexico City, but since that time he has always maintained a residence in Veracruz, and he confesses a dual allegiance that is observable in his writing.

Carballido began writing at an early age, primarily poems, stories and plays. In 1946 he began to write, "in earnest," and within two years he was an author with published and performed plays to his credit. A number of teachers were influential in the direction of his career. The playwrights Gorostiza and Novo contributed to his decision to write plays. Two additional literary figures of national reputation were important in the life of the young Carballido: the poet Carlos Pellicer, who was Carballido's teacher in the *secundaria,* and the novelist Augustín Yáñez, who taught Carballido grammar in the *preparatoria*. Carballido has said that the grammar class taught by Yáñez was the best class of his academic career.

The year 1950, like the period he spent with his father, was a turning point in Carballido's life. That year his only son, Juan de Dios Carballido Olalde, was born in Córdoba. Professionally, his first commercial productions, "La zona intermedia" and the monologue "Escribir, por ejemplo . . . ," opened the same day in different theaters. *Rosalba y los Llaveros*, which many critics still consider to be the best play, inaugurated the international season of the Institute of Fine Arts and the International Institute of Theater. And, finally, in 1950 he made his first trip outside Mexico, traveling to New York to study on a Rockefeller fellowship.

Following this decisive year, events began to happen very quickly for Carballido, though not all of them were affirmative. In 1958 *La sinfonía doméstica* closed following its premiere, an event Carballido called "something akin to the sinking of the Titanic." But that failure was followed in 1955 by a year of enormous success when he was appointed assistant director of the School of Theater at the University of Veracruz in Xalapa. He also wrote prolifically, publishing three major plays, a novella, and a collection of short stories. He attributes this productivity to being in Xalapa: "Xalapa did for me what Córdoba had done in 1939."

Following his first administrative appointment at Xalapa, Carballido has served as professor at the School of Dramatic Art of INBA, as a member of the editorial board of the University of Veracruz, as the director of cultural activities at that university, as director of the Department of Cultural Activities of the Polytechnic Institute, and as professor at the National University in Mexico City. He has been invited as honored guest by the governments of Japan, Cuba, and West Germany; he has traveled often in Cuba; he has acted as publicity director for the National Ballet as they toured Asia (an event Carballido cites as having given him his first major perspective on Mexico); he attended the highly successful performance of his "Yo, también, hablo de la rosa" in France; and has served on numbers of panels and juries of theater festivals throughout Latin America.

In the United States Carballido has been visiting professor at the Universities of Rutgers, Pittsburgh, and California. Recently Carballido's activities have been largely administrative, but in 1977 he resigned from all administrative responsibilities to be able to devote more time to writing.

Carballido lists many influences in his writing; among the strongest, personal and family experiences. The ex-convento of Santo Domingo, for example, in which he lived during the year with his father, figures prominently in several of his short stories and plays. The family pieces like "La desterrada," "Los huéspedes," *La danza que sueña la tortuga,* and *Un vals sin fin sobre el planeta,* reveal these influences. Carballido cites the influence of Jean Giraudoux in his reinterpretations of Greek myth, *Teseo* and *Medusa.* Other playwrights he considers major in his development are Arthur Miller, Tennessee Williams (especially *A Streetcar Named Desire*), Jean Anouilh, Sor Juana Inés de la Cruz, and "all of French theater and German expressionism." Carballido is a voracious reader, a student of world literature, but with the possible exception of Williams and their similar preoccupation with the theme of the wasted life, it would be difficult to say that Carballido owes very much to any writer, in spite of his easy acknowledgments of writers who have been important to him.

Carballido does not belong to any school or group of writers. Of his own generation his closest associates are Sergio Magaña and Luisa Josefina Hernández, who were fellow students with Carballido under the tutelage of Rudolfo Usigli, and Sergio Galindo, who was closely associated with Carballido in the publication of *La Palabra y el Hombre,* a review sponsored by the University of Xalapa. One sees certain thematic and tonal similarities among the four, but it is still more accurate to conclude that their ties are more personal than literary. Carballido truly is an independent author, a man with a very personal voice.

CHAPTER 2

Thirty-Three One-Act Plays

EMILIO Carballido's first successful writing was in the form of the one-act play. Although it is not unusual to find a young author attempting the short forms first, we may assume in Carballido's case that the motivation was not uncertainty or lack of confidence. From the beginning of his career, through his period of experimentation, and including his more mature writing, Carballido has always shown a marked preference for the briefer forms.

This prolific and talented Mexican writer has made solid contributions in many areas of literary endeavor. In addition to one-act plays, he has written full-length plays, librettos, the thematic line for ballets, screenplays, reviews, literary criticism, and prose fiction. The only major field in which he has not made an appreciable contribution is that of poetry.

Carballido has written thirty-three one-act plays, too many, spread over too long a timespan, to be explained away as the experimentation of a beginner. Even his full-length dramas tend to be brief. He has published a collection of short stories. Three of his four novels are, by English-language standards, novellas. The slightly longer novel is subtitled "A Romantic Fueilleton in XV Parts," and is essentially a series of brief episodes strung together in serialized form. In a recent interview Carballido characterized it as "a nineteenth century serial story in which every chapter advances events in the plot and the mystery."[1]

Mention of Carballido's preference for conciseness in expression is not intended as criticism; simply, it is prudent to observe that quantity is not tantamount to excellence. Consciously or unconsciously, Carballido has correctly assessed his particular talent for writing prose that suggests a great deal more than it

26

states; his best plays are extremely dense, in the sense that poetry is dense. Carballido is a demonstrative rather than a directive writer. He suggests and presents; rarely does he weigh or assess. It is seldom that one finds a trace of author comment in Carballido's writing. These rare instances are most often found in his earliest and most tentative pieces—or, and rarely, in a piece of social criticism that is explicitly didactic. Carballido realizes the value of allowing his audience to claim as its own the conclusions that he wishes to be drawn. For there are morals, lessons, and criticism in his work. Carballido is a man who is too little satisfied with the universal human condition and the sociopolitical situation in his own country to avoid problems in his writing; he has a great deal to say, and it is to his credit that he has said it with intelligent restraint.

We may note that his early plays may be categorized as either realistic or fantastic. Many articles of criticism on Carballido mention this obvious schism in the author's drama. This was at one time an accurate distinction, but one applicable only to the early period of his career. Later Carballido was to blend the realistic and fantastic in a style that has become the hallmark of his most accomplished drama; we can no longer speak of realism as opposed to fantasy. One group of one-act plays does fall within the definition of traditional realism, in content and in treatment. But in considering all the one-acts to date, many are best described as *non*realistic; that is, at times they may be surreal or gothic, they may be Pirandellian in their interruption of the fictional "reality" of theater, or they may be collages or spectaculars or pure fantasy. But these plays do *not* depict traditionally realistic events within a traditional time structure.

At his best, Carballido, like many writers throughout literary history, illustrates that the real and the nonreal do not necessarily form a dichotomy; rather, what we call fiction and what we call reality are often mirror images of the same truth. That demarcation is difficult, at times impossible, to distinguish. The symbology of the mirror in the twentieth century is so common as to have become trite. The question of what is real and what image is, nevertheless, an integral value in Carballido's canon, as witnessed in a footnote to one of his earliest one-act plays,

"La medalla," later revised and included in the first two volumes of *D.F.* In this sarcastic footnote which expresses his bitterness against censorship more explicitly than he usually allows himself within the body of a work, Carballido says: "Since the press, the radio, and the television convince the entire population that our realities are only fictions, must we writers always demonstrate how our fictions correspond to reality?" Though this statement has a specifically political application, it may also be read as a basic comment on the interrelationship between fiction and reality. This confusion, or more accurately, this acceptance of the fusion between reality and fiction, is one explanation of why things so often seem to be happening simultaneously, on two planes, in even the most "realistic" of Carballido's writing, and it is also why an arbitrary classification of realistic or fantastic is no longer a viable approach to a discussion of his work.

I *The First Plays: Steps Toward a Style*

Carballido wrote seven plays before the publication and performance of the three-act play *Rosalba y los Llaveros* in 1950. Because of the continuing success of *Rosalba,* and because it was chosen to inaugurate the international season at the Theater of the Bellas Artes, we can consider the performance a signal occasion, the first real recognition of Carballido as a major figure in Mexican drama. The seven plays written before that important year, then, quite naturally comprise a body of tentative steps toward a form and a discipline. Of those seven plays, six are one-acts. Two, *Los dos mundos de Alberta* (a three-act play to be discussed in a later chapter), and "El vestíbulo," have never been mentioned in any critical essay or bibliography of Carballido's work. Of them he says: "I intend never to publish them, but I have a great deal of affection for them."[2]

"El vestíbulo,"[3] Carballido's first one-act play, is typical of a style he was to develop in many of his short, and a few of his longer, plays. The lobby of the title is a hotel lobby, mysterious, and dark to the point of murkiness. The characters are not named—a technique often employed in the early plays—but called, simply, "He," "The Other," or "The Woman in Gray." The sense of mystery is augmented by a "Hotelkeeper" who is seen only as a silhouette, and a disembodied voice belonging to "The Figure."

The dark and mysterious tone is appropriate to the action. We learn that "The Lobby" is the anteroom to death. Through the visitations of several women—in gray, in green, in lilac—"He" reviews his past, all that he has lost, all that he denied himself. "The Figure," feminine in this embodiment, is his alter ego, or his ego, some presence that has always stood between him and successful intercourse with other humans. When "He" realizes he has lost everything except "The Figure," he attempts to seize her, but finds that all he holds in his hands is a deep-purple veil. The ending to this brief piece is metaphysical and mysterious. The clock strikes eight. The silhouette of the Hotelkeeper appears in the doorway: to the question by "He," "Is it time?" the hotelkeeper replies, "It is time" (14). But when "He" attempts to follow, he finds the doorway blocked by a mirror. Nothing is reflected there but his own image. No exit. And as the light fades from his upturned face, he is saying, "I don't understand."

"El vestíbulo" is not an accomplished dramatic work. Carballido himself, as noted, has no desire to publish the play. What is interesting is that here are themes and tones we will recognize in many of the plays of the first years of Carballido's career, particularly in the one-acts. In contrast, the first *three*-act plays are realistic comedies about the provinces. In passing one might note that this same pattern—metaphysical or mysterious one-acts, three-act comedies of manners—was followed by an earlier Mexican author, Xavier Villaurrutia, and although Carballido has never mentioned Villaurrutia as a primary influence in his work, he was very much present in the world of theater during Carballido's formative years.

"El triángulo sutil, una farsa para esnobs en un acto,"[4] is a little piece more accurately characterized as a conceit rather than a play. It is basically an idea, rather than a drama, and like a baroque conceit, it carries within it a deception that is revealed only in the last line of the play.

The tone, as one is informed by the subtitle, is self-consciously clever. Carballido frequently uses the word "subtle" in the body of the play to reflect the "subtle" of the title, and in the final line, he ironically emphasizes the subtlety of the entire concept. The setting of this "Triangle" is a very elegant bachelor's apartment. Raul and Sergio are two points of the triangle. The third point, as one might expect, is a woman referred to only as "She." Because the play is very dense, and extremely brief, every word is explicit. To summarize "Triángulo" is practically to recapitulate the action, but, as briefly as possible, two "sophisticated" young men, both lovers of—although not in love with— the same young woman, attempt to find a way to spare this very *sensitive* girl the knowledge that each of her lovers knows about the other. The only "satisfactory" solution for these elegant and exquisite sensibilities (Carballido is very conscious of his irony) is that one of the two lovers must die. Nobly, and gallantly, with refinement and delicacy, each offers to be the other's victim. Neither can accept the offer. They decide that poison will be the tool; poison demands no attacker/victim relationship. Both will take the poison, and *nature* will decide which is to die, through the simple expedient of establishing which body can least tolerate the toxin. Sergio leaves the apartment to buy the poison. Raul puts on a record, but before he can settle down to await Sergio's return, Sergio staggers back into the room, a large butcher knife protruding grotesquely from his chest.

> RAUL: What has happened to you? What is this? (He pulls the knife from Sergio's chest and stares at him with horror.)
> SERGIO: It was she, don't you see? She has another lover. He heard everything, outside. But he . . . isn't . . . subtle. (Dies) (186)

The conceit, of course, is that the subtle triangle of the title is not the standard two-male-one-female, but rather, the "surprise" symmetry of *three* lovers, each of whose triangle is tangential at the point represented by "She." The conceit of the subtle triangle is its *raison d'etre*: it is idea given substance, rather than drama employing ideas.

"La zona intermedia" was Carballido's first published work, appearing in 1949 in *América, Revista Antológica,* and also published later as a prologue to the *auto,*[5] "La triple porfía," followed by the unrelated monologue "Escribir, por ejemplo. . . ."

Charming is a damning word to apply to a work of art, and

yet it is precisely the word that describes "La zona intermedia."[6] The curtain opens on a scene of an intricate instrument panel manned by two "Assistants" absorbed in the task of "bringing up" the dawn, loosing the morning breezes, and regulating the accompanying lighting and musical effects. We are soon introduced to four characters who have been delayed in the intermediate zone because they are not yet fit to be judged by the Recording Angel. By the following definition they are *non*human: "Man can . . . do evil or good incidentally, unconsciously, like a weak little animal. Then he is lost. He has ceased to be a man" (31).

The most colorful of the four aspirants in the intermediate zone arrives: "A strange figure, a mixture of Cubist painting— with variations on the figure of a man—and Picasso's sculpture" (26). This creature is put through the "regenerator" by the astonished attendants, and when he emerges in his true form, he is a critic. A *nahual,* that protean animal figure of Mexican mythology, joins the group. He is there because the crucifix of a man he devoured has stuck in his throat. As he enters, the critic says: "What a curious mélange of pre-Columbian styles. Traces of the Teotichuacán, the Axtec . . . ," to which the refreshing *nahual* replies, "Mélange your old man!" (36).

The resolution of the Intermediate Zone is that each of the four candidates for divine judgment—a maiden, a fallen woman, an ineffectual little man, and the critic—is dispatched to an eternity befitting his particular sins and character. The *nahual,* because of an act of commitment performed while in the Zone, is converted into a human being and sent back to earth with the privileges *and* the responsibilities of a human being.

"La zona intermedia" is entertaining, full of charm and humor— the first of Carballido's plays to exhibit the humor so uniquely his. In a serious vein, Carballido has intelligent things to say about man's responsibilities in life. Unfortunately, the framework over which the humor and fantasy are draped is a little too apparent. The dialogue between the critic and the First Assistant disintegrates into a philosophical dialogue. When the Angel explains his coming role as a human to the *nahual,* the explanation is obtrusive; the symbolic action the *nahual* performed speaks for itself. We can appreciate the fact, however, that "La zona intermedia" is the work of an author still testing his style, and be a little less regretful that it is *almost* a perfect little play.

"La triple porfía"[7] is an appropriate companion piece to "La zona intermedia," as it, too, treats the question of responsibility, and, similarly, treats this problem with humor. A man called "He" returns to the home where his sweetheart died of a knife wound suffered during a lovers' quarrel. Where does the responsibility for this death lie? "He" is visited by three figures, an Angel, a Devil, and Reason. Theirs are the three arguments of the title; each offers a different solution to the anguish resulting from the lover's death. The Devil argues for suicide, and the oblivion of eternal shadows. The Angel believes "He" must suffer, and accept responsibility for the death. Reason suggests a practical solution: "Get your things and get out of town for a while until everything gets straightened out" (18).

"He" never has to face the responsibility, or the privilege, if one prefers, of making a choice. The police arrive to take him to jail. Reason departs to arrange bail. As everyone exits, the Angel, in very friendly fashion, accompanies the Devil: "He offers her his arm. She accepts" (18). Cynical? Perhaps. For the moment "He" has escaped. But he, like every human, will be accompanied by his three "graces." Carballido has opened a very large question in this very small play. It is an attractive exercise.

"El suplicante"[8] was performed in 1950 and published in 1958 in the *Revista de la Universidad de México* under the coauthorship of Carballido and Sergio Magaña. Carballido has disclaimed any major contribution to this very brief play, saying that he merely assisted Magaña with a few details. Since one cannot be certain exactly to what degree Carballido "assisted in the details" of "El suplicante," it is included here for two reasons: first, because this study attempts to follow the complete trajectory of Carballido's writing, and second, because of a particularly interesting aspect of the work. The play recounts a brief period in the incestuous love between a brother and a sister, and their relationship with a male friend who is in love with the sister. The play begins with a Director's announcement that two of Sor Juana Inés de la Cruz's *sainetes*[9] will be performed in place of the originally scheduled program. The performance begins, but it is almost immediately interrupted by the sound of quarreling offstage. The Sor Juana piece is abandoned, and, under the guise of justifying to the audience the ending of the originally scheduled play, the last and controversial scene is played so that the audience may judge whether or not it is appropriate. The three actors, as in Tamayo y Baus's *Un drama nuevo,* assume their parts, playing the roles that are theirs in life, and the play ends as the author/brother, carrying the action beyond the limits of the play-reality, kills his rival for his sister's love.

"El suplicante" as a whole is not successful. Its flaw is that midway through the play there is a major, and disastrous, change of tone; what begins as a farce ends very seriously. But for a student following Carballido's career, what is intriguing is that Carballido will employ the device of assuming the life-role within the fiction of the play in two later works: in one, "La fonda de las siete cabrillas," the device is used comically; in the second, the chilling and macabre one-act "La bodega," the effect is totally different.

Testimony to the fact that any divisions, temporal or thematic or stylistic, present anomalies, "Medalla al mérito"[10] reflects a much greater maturity of concept and style than the other plays discussed in this grouping. Were the didacticism expunged from "La zona intermedia," it would be equally excellent, but, as it stands, "Medalla" is the best of Carballido's early plays.

To say that "Medalla" is nonrealistic would seem at first glance to be misleading, for on one level it is a completely realistic account of a sordid and distasteful marriage. But here, the second level of action mentioned in the introductory remarks to this chapter is of prime importance. It is the dramatic line that develops above and outside the world perceived as "real" that lends the true dimension to this work. It is the use of the nonreal to enforce or magnify the world of reality-as-we-know-it that has resulted in much of Carballido's most effective drama.

Ignacio Robles is a Walter Mitty character who wants with all his heart to be the man he envisions in his fantasies. When he receives a medal for ten years of distinguished service at the bank where he is employed, he hopes this honor will reveal his true worth to the wife who has been too selfish and too blind to acknowledge it. He does enjoy her admiration, but, unfortunately, only in his fantasy. Also in his dreamworld, Ignacio sees himself pursued by a beautiful girl who finds him (and the money they have stolen from the bank's vault) so irresistible that she wants to run away with him. But wife Julia invades both his real and his imaginary worlds, harassing him, goading him to the breaking point. Master in his fancy, he tells her: "Get out of here, you pig. You're an idiot. Take that, and that, and that! I wish you were dead. (And she dies)" (132).

As a parallel to this fictitious scene, in the real world Ignacio looks at Julia with true hatred. He crushes the newspaper he has been reading and slowly and menacingly walks toward her. Julia watches.

"You're wrinkling the newspaper, and I haven't read it yet. Don't you hear me? You're going to tear it. (*Deliberately, he rips the newspaper into shreds. Then he bursts into sobs.*) "But Ignacio, for God's sake, what is the matter with you?" (*She rises and puts her arms around him. He, inconsolable, sobs upon her shoulder. Julia, tender, disconcerted, caresses him as one would a baby.*) "But can anyone tell me what's going on? What is the matter with this man?" (132)

These last moments are indicative of Carballido's innate sense of drama. He avoids the natural temptation to effect the neat parallel. The man brave in his fancy is not brave in fact. Too, he cleverly avoids making Julia the complete villainess. This restraint, this discipline in checking the forward thrust of an idea, distinguishes "Medalla" from the other early plays.

II   *The Monologues: Vehicles for Acting Students*

The monologue is a demanding dramatic form. Because of its abuse by decades of declaimers, the contemporary theatergoer has probably never seen a monologue performed. But because of his continuing association (since 1954) with schools of drama, Carballido has often written with the needs of theater students in mind. One of his specific purposes has been "to offer acting students material for their examinations." And perhaps for aspiring actors the shortcomings of the monologue are also its virtues: it is brief, inexpensive to produce, and it offers opportunities for an acting *tour de force.*

A student of theater is aware that one of the major difficulties in composing a monologue is to create a credible situation in which it seems natural for a person to stand alone before the audience. Carballido handles this problem adroitly. In "Escribir, por ejemplo," he employs the device of the telephone. In "Selaginela" there are several devices: a teenage girl sent to her room (1) shouts at her mother on the other side of the door, (2) enumerates grievances against a friend who has disappointed her as she punches holes in his picture, (3) recites parts of her school assignments, and (4) lovingly reads aloud the latest entry in a journal recording her fantasy encounters with her botany teacher. The invisible audience of "Las Parásitas" is a dead husband whose shade is being invoked. The audience, or "listener," in "Hipólito" is a model sitting for a painter. One assumes that the model is alive, but it is actually a bust; Hippolytus is rehearsing a speech he intends for his stepmother. The speaker in "Antes cruzábamos ríos" uses that most classic of monologue forms, the soliloquy. "La perfecta casada" is not, strictly speaking, a monologue; some half-dozen lines are spoken by other characters. In feeling and effect, however, it is so completely a one-character play that it is included here with the monologues.

Two of these plays are about teenagers. Both portray the loneliness, frustration, and easy despair so typical of the awkward years. Neither, however, leaves a tragic aftertaste. "Escribir, por ejemplo,"[11] shows a young poseur who likes to think of himself as a poet. Ernesto languishes in his room, testing his love letters and poetry on a friend at the other end of the telephone; meanwhile, the more enterprising friend has already made a date with the object of Ernesto's affections. Ernesto hangs up; he rages and weeps, but he *saves* the poem he was about to destroy. Ernesto will survive.

Similarly, in "Selaginela,"[12] Carballido demonstrates the tenacity of adolescents by drawing a parallel between the *selaginela* and the girl Ophelia. As Ophelia reads the description of the plant from her botany text, even she is eventually struck by a certain similarity. Carballido's game is apparent in a comparison of the following lines:

The selaginela

... then taking on the aspect of a small green fern. (32)

During the reproductive season, small organs, reddish in color, appear on the upper part of the fronds. (32)

During the dry season with the constant rays of the sun they acquire a golden tint, thus the name ... "leaves of gold." (32)

Ophelia

She is wearing a high school uniform, parrot green. (27)

Her face is covered with little pimples and blackheads, like constellations of little red points. (27)

(*She sits down at the window and looks outside. The sun turns her body gold.* (33)

Carballido illustrates, optimistically, that in spite of her very real pain, Ophelia will survive like her counterpart the *selaginela*, which "demonstrates the peculiarity of resisting long periods of drought..." (32).

In "Parásitas"[13] Carballido again draws a parallel between the human and plant worlds, but in this play specific identification is more difficult; at times the parasite would seem to be the wife, at others, the husband. Since the husband is dead, it would follow that the still-living wife is the parasite, feeding from the memory—the dead trunk—of her husband. This point of view is substantiated when Sweet Mary, the wife, says of an actual tree in the patio outside her window: "The tree is completely dry now. The parasitical plants are still living.... I would like to paint something like that: the principle life is dead, the trunk is dead, but the poor parasite still clings to it" (151). But the obvious is contradicted when Sweet Mary, perhaps trying to convince herself that life is easier without her husband, reminisces about how she sacrificed her own aspirations to satisfy her husband's eccentric demands: "*Your* things, *your* life. I was the trunk, you were the parasite" (155).

"Las parásitas" is a potentially fascinating piece, but the reader, in attempting to distinguish the host from the feeder, may find himself in the position of the wife who in the closing lines of the play "sits pensively, not understanding" (156). The ultimate, though not entirely satisfying, solution may be found in the plural title: both Sweet Mary and her husband are parasites, and both—though botanically impossible—the hosts.

Of the six monologues written by Carballido, "La perfecta casada"[14] is much the most exciting dramatically. In it a woman accompanied by her young child comes to a police station to "stand by" a husband who is under arrest for the murder of his mistress. She illustrates her perfection as she primps before the photographer and vents her destructive powers upon her child.

What unfolds between the lines in "La perfecta casada" is a portrait, a *self*-portrait, of a shrew. The beauty of this portrait consists of the ingenious duality so effectively employed by Carballido. On the surface, in the literal sense of the words, the "perfect" wife says nothing to mar the image of a virtuous, long-suffering, faithful wife and mother. But ingeniously, her words create a more incriminating picture than another person ever could. When the husband is shown into the visiting room, his silence and his frantic attempts to escape the very presence of his wife specifically illustrate the tension and electricity of this monologue. Carballido has created a monologue with real dramatic intensity in "La perfecta casada."

"Antes cruzábamos ríos,"[15] written a decade after the preceding monologues, remains similar in tone to the earliest of them. While this monologue is spoken by a very old man—in contrast to the teenage protagonists of the earlier pieces—"Antes cruzábamos ríos," like them, contemplates a relatively brief moment of pain, disillusion, and despair; like them, too, it ends on an optimistic note. Esteban, a half-blind elderly farmer, shoots his son's dog, mistaking it for a rabbit. His monologue is a lament, a nostalgia for the days when "there used to be rivers" and animals and space instead of the highways and buildings now occupying land that once was his. Esteban is fearful of his son's reaction to the dog's death, and he is saddened by his grandchildren's lack of respect for him. He is tempted to shoot himself and end an existence that has become meaningless. But a simple sound, the call of a lark, convinces him that life is worthwhile.

The openly sentimental tone of "Antes cruzábamos ríos" is

apparent from the preceding summary, and although it is perhaps an interesting exercise for an actor, it does not contribute substantially to Carballido's stature as a dramatist.

III The Realistic One-Act Plays: Mexico City Vignettes

Carballido's collection of one-act plays, entitled D.F. (Federal District, referring to Mexico City)) was first published in 1957. It contained nine plays: the first four of the monologues previously discussed and "El Censo," "Misa primera," "El espejo," "Tangentes," and "Medalla al mérito." In 1962 an augmented edition was published which contained eight of the nine plays of the first edition ("Hipólito" was omitted) plus five new plays: "La perfecta casada" (discussed in the section dealing with monologues), "Paso de madrugada," "El solitario en octubre," "Un cuento de Navidad," and "Pastores de la ciudad."

A third edition (the penultimate, the most recent was published in 1977) in 1973 contains the same number of plays. However, "El espejo" and "Medalla al mérito" have been omitted and "Delicioso domingo" and "Una rosa con otro nombre" have been substituted for them. The reason for this change is that Carballido intended to include the nonrealistic "El espejo" and "Medalla" in the later collection. The result is an entirely realistic third edition of D.F. With realistic and nonrealistic categories so clearly established, we can consider the remaining one-act plays in those two groupings.

Communicating necessary information about the situation at a play's opening can be intrusive and annoying in the brief piece. This is a failing Carballido consistently avoids with grace in his one-act plays. One way he manages to avoid annoying exposition is by constructing plays that exist within their own action, and to which outside events have little or no relevance. D.F. states as one of its purposes: "To make a dramatic collage, a kaleidoscope of little actions with the goal of painting the author's very personal visions of his Federal District."[16] As a result, many of the realistic plays portray moments of encounter, chance meetings, tangential relationships; they focus on an accidental present that has no relation to the past—although it may affect the future. These are skillful snapshots of the infinite possibilities of the drama inherent in the constantly shifting human relationships of any city, a format that has been explored by countless writers. Social criticism is often a theme in these works. This social comment ranges from the general, marriage-as-the-thing-to-do, in "El solitario en octubre"; the specific—the police force—in "Paso de madrugada" and "Un cuento de Navidad"; and nonsensical governmental action, in "El censo."

Four of these realistic plays focus on serious personal relationships. "Primera misa" tells of a maiden lady whose hunger for affection makes her susceptible to strays—animal or human. "Tangentes" presents the tragedy of the wasted lives of two elderly people and the questionable stability of a love affair between two young people. "El solitario en octubre" portrays the banality of a relationship based on a desire for all the symbols of material and marital success. And "Una rosa, con otro nombre"[17] describes a dancehall encounter between an upper-class youth "on the make," and a lower-class girl who is pregnant and searching for someone she can trick into believing he is the father of her unborn child. Of these four plays, "El solitario en octubre" is the most convincing, presenting the very human indecision, frustration, and tragedy of persons who do not themselves understand the reasons for their actions.

The four remaining realistic one-acts are similar in situation and character to the first four, but there is a large difference between them: now the tone becomes comic. "El Censo" depicts a government census taker who changes from menace to accomplice as everyone involved frantically contrives to falsify documents to meet the demands of the census taker's daily quota. "Paso de madrugada" features two policemen whose criminal indifference to the pleas of a man attempting to get his pregnant wife to the hospital changes to Keystone slapstick when they fear the wife is about to deliver her child in their station. "Un cuento de Navidad" effectively underscores differences in social conditions, contrasting the figure of a department store Santa Claus hired to have his picture taken with the children of affluent clients with that of a scruffy, pinned-together scarecrow of a Santa and an incompetent photographer who have come to work the same beat. "Delicioso domingo" introduces the reader to Magda and Chuchis, two rather shopworn "ladies of the night" and to their efforts, primarily based on self-deceit, to spend a "swell Sunday" in Chapultepec Park.

Finally, two realistic pieces, not included in *D.F.*, are more difficult to define. One is "Las noticias del día,"[18] which is perhaps most accurately described as a "mini-spectacular." It is a re-creation of news stories, features, and want ads being read by a man awaiting a rendezvous with his sweetheart. The tenuous story line is far outweighed by the play's concept, though this technique of making the printed page reality is used with even greater imagination in "La bodega." "Noticias," too, has comic moments: for example, brides of all shapes and sizes—including one about eight months pregnant—emerging from the society page. The second piece, "El fin de un idilio,"[19] was written in honor of the hundred-year anniversary of Amado Nervo's birth, and incorporates quotations from Nervo's work into the account of a juvenile love affair.

Each of *these* realistic plays is humorous, and many are specifically reliant on visual humor: burlesque policemen, the drunken and soaking-wet Magda and Chuchis dumped into the lake during a scuffle between their "escorts" and a boatload of university students, a scruffy Santa Claus, love-sick fourteen year olds, and pregnant brides. Notable, too, is the fact that all these realistic plays concern themselves with the disadvantaged. Each of these characters, harassed and hassled by society, by life itself, is totally sympathetic and completely outside any moralistic criticism. These are very funny plays, and their style is uniquely Carballido. There is no other Latin American writer who can be more comic, and at the same time more touching.

IV   *Two Spectaculars: History—Real and Literary*

In 1968 Carballido wrote "El Almanaque de Juárez,"[20] an epic drama that was performed in Mexico City in 1969 and again three years later in Nuevo Leon in celebration of the centenary of Juarez's death. This one-act spectacular reviews the story of Juarez' life, his humble origins, his enormous capacity for learning, his marriage with a woman of superior social status, his military and political careers, and ends with a resume by the patriotic figure of the mother country of his influence and impact on the nation of Mexico.

The most notable aspect of "El Almanaque de Juárez" (aside from its obvious political and social import and the imparting of little-known facts, for example, that Mexico instituted a system of public education years before France or England [26]) is Carballido's use of "flowing" or "running" time. This device allows the actors to move through time as they are speaking; exposition and action exist simultaneously, and time moves as if the audience were watching a speeded-up film. As an example, as Juarez is speaking with his sister Josefa, nursemaid to the infant Margarita who will in time become Juarez' wife, four years pass in the space of a few lines, from a reference to a baby girl "born yesterday," to news of Margarita's fourth birthday only six speeches later.

Carballido uses this technique throughout the piece, and so in the space of some thirty manuscript pages, he depicts the major events of Juarez' personal and political life as well as the broader, though closely related, events of a nation's history over the span of a half-century.

"El Almanaque de Juárez" is a representative showcase of several of Carballido's devices and themes. In addition to his always adept treatment of time, a recurring characteristic is his inclination to correlate ordinary occurrences with essences in a kind of poetic treatment most familiar, perhaps, in the roles of the Lecturer and the Intermediary in "Yo también hablo de la rosa." In the "Rosa," the Lecturer analyzes the psychological and sociological explanations of human behavior by using the example of the rose: to the psychologist the essence of the rose is the individual petal. To the sociologist, the essence lies in the whole, the petals have no meaning except in their contribution to the whole rose. The Lecturer finally suggests that the essence of the rose may best be found in the "web," the "fabric," and "union of cells" that comprise the rose, a viewpoint echoed by the Intermediary. Similarly, in the Juarez play, Carballido defines history by employing the example of a simpler figure. History is likened to the process of photography: "a phenomenon of lights and shadows and salts that 'fix' isolated actions in order to store them in a collective memory. The light that emanates from a man's actions serves to fix those actions, to leave us an enduring image. . . . Although shadow also photographs and per-

petuates certain figures. Very fuzzy at times, like this one. ...."
(5–6)

The mention of poetic treatment used to describe Carballido's
explanation of the process of history is not inappropriate in
describing other portions of the play. In one scene, Carballido
has borrowed directly from Shakespeare's *Othello*. As Margarita
and Juarez enact a scene portraying Margarita's transition from
childhood to adulthood, as Juarez courts her and wins her, the
Photographer (still the poetic voice) recites Othello's monologue
that begins: "Her father loved me, yes oft invited me; Still ques-
tioned me the story of my life."[21] The monologue ends with
these lines (and Carballido isolates them in the text): "She
loved me for the dangers I had passed, And I loved her that
she did pity them." The lines that follow in Shakespeare, "Here
comes the lady. . .," serve as a bridge in the Carballido spectacular, connecting the Shakespeare allusion with the opening
lines of a Mexican song: "Here comes the girl that I adore."[22]
Though the monologue is written in prose form, its poetic origin
is underscored in the manuscript copy by slash marks indicating
poetic lines (10–11).

As the Photographer recalls the Intermediary in "La rosa,"
the treatment of the historical period of the French intervention
in this spectacular recalls the play *Las cartas de Mozart*. The
ladies who insist on intruding into the historical narrative, wanting to speed it up so they can see the part about their "darling
Max and Carlotita," are direct prototypes for Malvina and
Renata in the 1974 play.

Finally, the character of "The Mother Country," whose monologue closes the action of "El Almanaque de Juárez" is quintes-
sentially a Carballido invention. She enters the stage giggling and
arranging her flowing robes: "It always makes me laugh when
they put a Liberty cap and a tricolor robe on some little school-
girl and pretend that she's the mother country. And now, the
teacher's chosen me and I have to come out here looking like
this" (24). But as she recites her memorized lines she is transformed, and by the end of the speech she is openly weeping,
swept by patriotic feeling.

Carballido thus moves from comedy to patriotism without

ever slipping into bathos. "El Almanaque de Juárez" is a sincerely moving tribute to one of Mexico's greatest heroes.

A second Carballido spectacular, "La fonda de las siete cabrillas,"[23] is based on a play by the nineteenth-century Mexican playwright Manuel Eduardo de Gorostiza. In a "preamble to be printed on the theater program," Carballido explains the genesis of the work. He had been commissioned by the government to write some one-act plays intended for a "popular" audience. When these plays were rejected and the director with whom he was working, Guilaumín, was requested to produce instead a work by an author more appropriate for the "people," the result was Carballido's adaptation of *Don Bonifacio*. "I proceeded," says Carballido, "to revise the original text which is marked by haste and an increasing lack of zest, but which opens itself to theatrical possibilities that Pirandello was to explore in depth" (50). And, although Carballido has experimented in other places with a Pirandellian interruption of theatrical illusion, this work surely is representative of what is not only Pirandello's, but typically a late twentieth-century concern: experimentation with the intrusion of reality into the illusion of fiction.

The plot of the play is that of classic farce, and the characters are those demanded by that genre: a deceitful husband (Don Roque); a deceived wife (Doña Cándida); a long-lost suitor (Don Silvestre) who returns in time to console the wife; an attractive woman of questionable virtue (Doña Luz) who is more than willing to entertain the roving husband; and the cast is rounded out by an assortment of family members and servants who add spice to the farcical stew. The four principal characters come together at the Inn of the Seven Kids. The humorous/amorous complications develop predictably, but entertainingly, until Don Bonifacio, the protagonist of the nineteenth century play, bursts onto the stage to interrupt the action. This gentleman cannot tolerate the cavortings of the actress playing Doña Luz, who happens to be his wife; he will not permit her to behave in such a scandalous manner; the play must not continue. Naturally, there are protests from the audience, and at least two, Juan and Josefa, demand their money back. A solution is suggested: they will try two endings, the

original—which Don Bonifacio considers immoral—and a second
written by him in which every character repents of his wrong-
doing; the audience will decide which ending is more fitting.
After the alternative endings are enacted, Juan and Josefa are
still dissatisfied, and they propose a *third* version which ends
to everyone's satisfaction:

JUAN: Everyone's happy, even us.
JOSEFA: Even us. (Murmurs) Let's go home now.
JUAN: Right. All that's missing is a little music.

As everyone, including the audience, joins in the singing and
dancing, the spectacular ends.

In this play Carballido is at his most purposefully entertaining. Comedy, of course, is a constant in his theater, even
in the plays of serious intent, but in this instance comedy is
at the service of comedy. Up-beat and frivolous, "La fonda de
las siete cabrillas" is the work of a very puckish Carballido.

V Political Realism: A Short Day's Anger

"Un pequeño diá de ira"[24] was published in Cuba in 1962
where it won the Casa de las Américas award for the best
play of that year. In its pronounced emphasis on class consciousness, its explicit criticism of the clergy and of governmental
authority, it is the most overtly political of Carballido's plays.
Once again one recognizes the extent of his social consciousness.

"Un pequeño diá de ira" begins on a quiet Sunday afternoon
in an ordinary small port city on the Gulf of Mexico. The
characters are introduced in successive small groups that break
away from the usual Sunday afternoon crowd that has gathered
in the plaza. It is very hot, and people are bored and vaguely
dissatisfied. We are immediately aware of the three distinct
levels of society in the village. The influential level includes
the mayor and the Vargases. Cristina Cifuentes de Vargas is
the wealthiest woman in the town, and the least liked. All the
children call her "the old witch." At a slightly inferior level
are the rich merchants represented by the Ruiz and the Avelar
families. The rest of the characters are of varying grades of

lower levels, bank clerks, maids, fishermen, school teachers, derelicts, and children. The action of the play develops on a line of rising hysteria. The innocent and aimless pranks of the children on this free, warm Sunday afternoon lead them to the mango trees of "the old witch" (this childhood innocence will be seen later in "Yo también haldo de la rosa"). Cristina, who is pregnant, and tired of the continual harassment of the children, fires a gun at them "to frighten them." One, Angel, is killed—struck between the eyes by a bullet. The ordinary townspeople, naturally, resent the accident and the preferential treatment Cristina receives from the mayor. Uneasiness and restlessness assume the form of rebellion and overt acts of rebellion. This potentially explosive situation is actually triggered by the arrest of the local madman. An aroused throng marches on the jail to free him. Infected with violence, the crowd runs out of control. They wreck Cristina's home, remove her from "house arrest" and lead her to the jail. They run the mayor and his cronies out of town, and pillage their homes. Violence exhausts itself, and the town returns to "normal." The last scene is a recapitulation of the first: "A Sunday like the one of the opening scene" (94). It is not the same town, however: "something has changed in this town" (95), and everyone knows it.

The very large cast includes a narrator who comments on the events from outside the action. It is at the end of the tenth section of the play, at the height of dramatic tension, that, surprisingly, the narrator breaks the convention of his position of impartiality and enters the action, a shocking dramatic effect.

Shouts of assent. Two men take Cristina by the arms. Onésimo starts to intervene, a push sends him to the other side of the room. Cristina shouts and cries out, but they remove her from the room. Everyone begins to leave. As a final flourish, women tear down the draperies, *and the narrator breaks some piece of furniture that still remains standing.* Everyone exits. (92)[25]

In the final scene the narrator once again steps outside the action of the play. He comments on the town's new officials. The townspeople talk among themselves. Since the upper stratum

represented by the mayor and other high officers has been run
out of town along with Cristina, the merchants and well-to-do
who now find themselves at the highest social level of the
community are uneasy about their new position. Having witnessed violence, they have every reason to believe in the
possibility of future violence, even though the appearance of
the town is now calm. The Narrator observes: "The fragile,
shimmering and tangled thread of individual lives is still un-
winding. But there was a short day's anger. Just a *short* day's
anger" (95). The final words, actually, are superfluous. The
implications are clear:

The Narrator walks away, begins to disappear in the crowd.
  NARRATOR: *There could be a long day's anger!*
He is lost among the people. Played loudly, the last lines of "Over
the Waves." (95)

VI *Nonconventional Plays: Horror, Myth, Poetry and Dream*

"Pastores de la ciudad" and "El espejo" complete the plays
contained in the first three editions of *D.F.* "El espejo" and
"Medalla al mérito," already mentioned in the group of Carballido's earliest plays, were omitted from the third edition
in order to be included in a separate collection. "Pastores de
la ciudad,"[26] like "Medalla al mérito" and "El espejo," actually
belongs in the nonrealistic collection. It does share with the
realistic plays the fact that it is a play of encounter, but
animals that talk and a policeman/devil-figure who vanishes in
clouds of smoke and brimstone must categorize this play as
nonliteral. Once again Carballido avoids the need for exposition
by almost immediately suggesting a recreation of the circum-
stances attending the birth of Christ. The folk belief in the
temporary amnesty in worldly problems, and the traditional
gathering of the animals and their humble keepers, are represented in this play. Also of interest to students of Mexican
literature is the inclusion of *villancicos*[27] composed by Sor Juana
Inés de la Cruz. The play is moving in its evocation of the
nostalgia of city-locked peasants for the lost paradise of the
old pastoral ways.

"El espejo"[28] is a small classic. A girl, Alda, stands before her mirror trying on various flowers, combs, and necklaces, but nothing gives the effect she desires. Her boy friend Héctor enters, and their conversation is testimony to the vulgarity of their relationship. Rubén arrives to escort Alda to the opera. Héctor has to hide under the bed; he does not want to frighten off the goose that lays the golden eggs. When Rubén enters, a new Alda is reflected in the mirror: "I look fine now, don't I?" Preparing to leave, they search for Alda's wrap. Rubén looks under the bed and sees Héctor. After a delayed reaction, Rubén comments that there is a man under the bed. Alda tries to convince Rubén that Héctor is the plumber. Another delayed reaction, and Rubén sadly faces reality. As he strikes Alda, one hears the sound of shattering glass: "*Rubén exits, and after him, walking or dragging themselves according to their nature, all the furniture and other objects exit from the room. The music, also. It ends with the exit of the curtains. The only thing remaining is the bed, its striped mattress exposed by the departure of the sheets and bedspread*" (79). Alda suggests to Héctor that they take advantage of the opera tickets that Rubén left behind in disgust. "Opera?" laughs Héctor in disbelief, and throws Alda on the bed. "El espejo" is a tiny play, but marvelously complete.

If they were short stories, the plays of the trilogy *El lugar y la hora*[29] would be called tales. They are macabre, consciously so, but at the same time haunting and beautiful. This is theater made from the stuff of dreams, and traditional criteria are insufficient to measure their beauty.

Two of the plays deal with an ordinarily taboo subject, necrophilia. "El amor muerto" treats a clandestine attraction between a stepfather and his daughter, both of whom are dead and slowly decomposing. In a horrible and fascinating scene, the girl's fiancé appears and tries to force her to return home with him. During the struggle he tugs at her arm, which separates from the socket and falls to the floor. As the girl laments this intrusion into their precious remaining moments, her lover tenderly caresses and soothes her: "Don't cry any more. Your eyes might fall out" (21).

"El glaciar" has strongly mythic overtones. This play recounts the story of an elderly lady who comes to the foot of a glacier to await the emergence of the ice-encased body of her fiancé who fifty years before on the day of their wedding had fallen into a crevasse. The old lady, entering a skin that has been preserved through the years with the body of the youth, temporarily returns to the past, and the two celebrate their unconsummated marriage. On the following morning, the youth's corpse is accompanied to a burial spot by the elderly lady and her present husband.

"La bodega" is as weird and compelling as its two companion pieces. An applicant for a salesman's position observes a demonstration of a very unusual product, *living* books. As the employer reads aloud, the action of the story being read is enacted by the life-size characters stored in large wooden crates stamped with book titles. Only books that have horrible and unnatural characters are kept in stock. The demonstration illustrates the unholy love affair between a monk and a beautiful girl. Their punishments: the girl gradually degenerates into an unrecognizable creature and the monk increasingly lusts after this abomination. Horror is compounded when it becomes apparent that the characters may be "read" only once, and that the young people who have come to inquire about a job are in reality replacements rather than applicants.

The trilogy *El lugar y la hora* represents the extreme in Carballido's experimentation with fantastic drama. What we see is the reality of horror, myth, poetry, cruelty and dream incorporated in effective and beautiful theater.

Quite a different form of fantasy is employed in "Teseo,"[30] Carballido's recreation of the Greek myth. Carballido faithfully conforms to the basic events of the legend, but the Theseus we meet is not the Greek hero we know. Like the Greek protagonist, this Theseus comes to Thebes and is welcomed lovingly by his father Aegeus. Theseus voyages to Crete, kills the minotaur, and, with Adriadna's help, escapes from the labyrinth. He returns to Thebes, where he becomes king. But Carballido (always working within the sequential events of the mythic prototype) has created a new Theseus, one completely removed from fatalistic determinism. The new Theseus's assumption of responsibility for his own conduct makes him immoral, even vicious; at the same time he is a man, and not a puppet of the gods.

Making his character responsible for his actions—actor rather than victim—Carballido creates a ruthless and cruel antihero; he uses every human contact to his own advantage, he discards those who have served their purpose, and he destroys any who stand in the way of his ambition. One knows from the myth that Aegeus will die and be replaced by his son; he leaps into the sea when he sights the ship returning from Crete under the black sails that signal the mission's failure—sails *accidentally* left unchanged. But Carballido's Theseus neither trusts nor relies on the gods:

TESEO: Raise the black sails.
CAPTAIN: The red ones, sir. Those of celebration.
TESEO: The black ones.
CAPTAIN: Your father will be waiting to see us appear on the horizon. The red ones.
TESEO: I said . . . the black ones. (Unsheathes his sword.) Did you hear?
CAPTAIN: Yes, sir. The . . . black ones. (672)

The difference in effect between the two versions demonstrates the amazing breach between responsibility for one's own acts and the comfortable security of god-directed action.

In the same scene, Carballido illustrates his density of style. He writes:

ARIADNA: The sea frightens me. I've been on shipboard only once and I was dreadfully seasick.
TESEO: There are islands on the way. If you feel bad, we can stop at Naxos and allow you to rest. Let's go.
FEDRA: I read in a travel book that Naxos is a horrible island. That pirates maroon people there. And there are wild animals. And. . . .
TESEO: (Puts his hand over her mouth): There are no wild animals on Naxos.
FEDRA: Don't smile like that, that's the way my father smiled. If you ever became like him. . . .
TESEO: Then what?
FEDRA: I don't know. . . . But I like young men. (672–73)

In these few lines, Carballido has suggested the whole continuity of the myth. Ariadna will be discarded, no longer useful or desired, on the island of Naxos. Theseus will accompany Heracles to the Amazons and there marry Antiope and engender Hippolytus. In his later years he will marry Phaedra, who betrays her husband Theseus in a love affair with his son. Following the myth, Carballido's Theseus will live the same events, but he will not be the same man.

"Yo también hablo de la rosa"[31] is the most important one-act play written by Carballido, and one of his best plays of any length. "La rosa," winner in Mexico of the best play award for 1967, has been translated into English and into French where it played to very good reviews in 1974. "La rosa" is an excellent example of the style that will be Carballido's most significant and most lasting contribution to theater.

The point of departure for "La rosa" is a strictly realistic incident, the derailment of a train by two hookey-playing children. The play is not *about* the train wreck, however. "La rosa" poses a question, "What is the quality of reality?" a question developed through the metaphor of "What is the essence of a rose?" At the same time, the play is an overt criticism of social forces at work both within and outside Mexico.

The scenes of the play are short and staccato, with rapid changes of location and subject. The changes are accomplished with blackouts, so that the effect is one of a series of images flashed upon the observer's consciousness, as if the fragments of the play were projected slides. The audience is made additionally aware of the ambiguous nature of reality, and of reality as it is represented on the stage, by the intermittent intrusions of the Intermediary, who is a commentator on, although she never directly alludes to, the realistic events being enacted. Except in the closing sequence, the Intermediary is completely outside the frame of the action taking place on stage, interrupting the illusion that is the essence of theater.

The longest segment of "La rosa" is composed of the events leading to the derailment of the train. The accident is presented as the natural result of the idle play of two youngsters with normal curiosity and with time on their hands. These two children roll a large, concrete-filled metal drum onto the railroad track—"just to see what will happen." This incident is subsequently reenacted three times during the play; the recreations are played in pantomime and narrated first by a psychologist, second by a sociologist, and last by the Intermediary. The reality of the happening changes with each observer.

On the level of social criticism Carballido attacks many villains: a school system that keeps children out of school by demanding conformity in dress; unsympathetic teachers; the difficulties of "widowed" mothers; the shallowness of certain academics; and Yankee imperialism. Criticism is an integral part of "La rosa." More important, however, is what happens on a symbolic level, based on two principal metaphors. The first relates the heart and its circulatory system to the origin and presence of knowledge. The second, and more important, figure uses the rose to illustrate properties of the human being in his society.

The first metaphor is most prominent in the opening and closing portions of the play. In her first speech, the Intermediary likens knowledge to the heart: "Hidden, beating, imperceptibly glowing, directing the functions of rhythmical canals that in their sistole and diastole lead to other canals, to torrents, to still unnoticed currents governed by the radiant complexity of a potent central valve..." (7). And the last words of the play contain the same allusions:

MAXIMINO: And now each of us . . .
TOÑA: . . . holding hands, linked together in this circle. . . .
POLO: . . . will hear. . . .
TOÑA: . . . for a long, long time. . . .
MAXIMINO: . . . the mystery. . . .
THE INTERMEDIARY: . . . of our own hearts. . . .
(*The dance, the chain, continues to weave its great circle as the lights come up, throbbing like heartbeats, to their greatest intensity.*) (22)

Through these references, Carballido proposes a mystical definition of knowledge; he intimates that knowledge possesses qualities of beat and diffusion, and that these qualities originate in the pulsing center of the universe, the human heart.

The metaphor of the rose is clarified in a sequence depicting a lecture illustrated by three enormous color photographs: one is of a red rose (a heart/rose relationship is difficult to deny), one a petal of that rose, and one a microscopic cross section of the petal. The material discussed in the lecture parallels the interpretations of the basic incident of the play. We see in the first reenactment of the trainwreck, narrated by the psychologist, that the petal represents man's condition:

Lecturer

First hypothesis: without the petal there is no rose. Watch this carefully: strip the petals, and what remains? There are no roses! They have never existed! There are only petals. (21)

First Professor:

Here is the nucleus: in the Ego. A complex ego composed of many layers wrapped one upon another, like ... like the petals of ... a rose. (16)

The *rose* represents the sociologist's view of the role of the individual:

Lecturer

Second hypothesis: The petal is nothing. When have you seen something grow that looks like this petal? From what stem would it grow? Who would ever notice if a petal were missing from a rose, or two, or three? There are no petals! There are only roses. (21)

Second Professor

The manifestations of the individual can be judged only in relation to his function in the collectivity. The isolated individual does not *exist*. We are social beings. (18)

The third version of the accident and the events leading up to it are narrated by the Intermediary. This version suggests reality as it is seen by mystics and poets. The newsboy who cries the news before each reenactment now carries newspapers printed on parchment or ámatl, and they are covered with magic signs as well as printed words. Ritual dance and music are employed in this third recreation. The noise of the crash is accompanied by the sound of happy laughter and music and colored lights. The accident becomes *l'acte gratuite*, the unmotivated act that some consider to constitute true liberty.

In this poetic and mystic interpretation of reality, the human entity is seen to be a compound of all things, a collection of universal cells, the cross section that the *Lecturer* uses to illustrate one of the images of the rose:

Lecturer

Third hypothesis: there are neither petals nor roses. There is merely a web, a fabric, a union of cells. Suppress that union, and there is nothing. That fabric is basic matter, living matter. And that matter is not matter, it is energy. There is no matter, there are no petals, there is no rose, there is no perfume, nothing! Only a homogeneity of miraculous fictions, and one is called "rose" and others are called by other names, one miracle after another, everywhere, with no possible rational explanation. (21)

The Intermediary

The children were becoming part of everything that surrounded them: they were the dump, the flowers, and they were clouds, amazement, pleasure, and they saw . . . and they understood . . . and that was all. (21)

"Yo también hablo de la rosa" is rich in the multiplicity of its metaphors. Carballido's answer to the question posed by the play, "What is the nature of reality?" is clear: To Carballido, reality is poetic.

These thirty-three one-act plays offer a comprehensive sampling of Carballido's talents as a dramatic writer. They run the gamut from realistic to fantastic (certainly, the macabre trilogy *El lugar y la hora* represents Carballido's most extreme experimentation with fantasy), and include excellent examples of the combination of realism and nonrealism that results in the author's best work. Perhaps the variety itself is the single most surprising factor in an overall consideration of the one-act plays. They offer a spectrum of modes and styles not matched in the more "major" plays. Carballido has demonstrated the broad potential for expression in this often-ignored dramatic form.

CHAPTER 3

Short Stories

THE collection *La caja vacía*[1] was published in 1962. Of the literary genres to which Carballido has contributed substantially—short and full-length plays, short story, and novel—this collection is his most homogeneous offering. Considering their quality, one wonders why Carballido has not returned to the short story form.

The ten stories of this collection establish the tone of a way of life. With one or two exceptions their setting is provincial Veracruz during an earlier generation. (This is also the time and the place of the novel *El sol,* and of the plays *Un vals sin fin sobre el planeta,* and *La danza que sueña la tortuga*). Most of the stories tell us that life is difficult, that good times are fleeting, and that perhaps Proust was right: happiness exists only in retrospect. Most describe family relationships, childhood reminiscences, and the ways one managed to exist in difficult times. Centering as they do about the hearth and the routine activities of living, the characters of *La caja vacía* are predominantly women and children. Men are largely peripheral to these stories. They are sustenance or menace to their household, but they are not integral to the story; they may act, but they are not acted upon.

I Two Male Protagonists: A Loser and a Winner

Two exceptions to the nonmale protagonist general rule are "Las conferencias," and "El cubilete." The least germane to the collection as a whole is "Las conferencias," and, perhaps not coincidentally, it is also the least effective story. Its protagonist is a foreign author-lecturer; the point of contact with the collection is the setting in Huatusco, a small provincial town which is one of the stops on an organized series of lectures. In this case,

the atmosphere of the village is not used to underline a mood
of familiar recognition but, conversely, to magnify the outsider's sense of isolation: "Something unidentifiable: the almost
rural sounds filtering into the room, the inevitably folksy—almost
folkloric—air of the rundown hotel ... something of all this,
perhaps all of it together, caused the man to suspend his writing and slowly raise his eyes from his work, as hazily he thought
'stranger, stranger' " (83). And by never giving the lecturer a
name, Carballido adds lack of identity to lack of recognition.

"Las conferencias" is a mood story without specific plot or
action. The lecture, and the audience response, are always the
same, with only minor variations. It is this sameness, the in-
tolerably repetitious mediocrity, that intensifies the lecturer's
state of extreme fatigue and loneliness. He has reached the point
where it is physically painful for him to deliver the same tiring
lecture day after day. He struggles on—cliché following cliché.
Time, he says, is a river in whose waters we may never dip
again, "a liquid in a porous flask trickling away drop by drop ..."
(88). Ironically, his own life is escaping in the same way, symbolically paralleled in drops of sweat that fall onto the few
notebooks opened for his autograph following his lecture. The
maestro cannot teach himself.

"El cubilete" is the only other story with a male protagonist.
Here, in a provincial town, we witness a routine day amid the
customary gathering of the village power elite, and specifically,
the day of a small-time hanger-on who hopes to curry favor
with the local boss. Mario, a cheap hustler, is quite different
from the quasi-intellectual lecturer of "Las conferencias," yet
there is something strangely similar about the two men. Both
are individuals who drift with the current, always looking for a
"deal." Neither has the strength, or, apparently, the desire, to
change the direction of his life. And both prey upon their
families: Mario, very concretely, by financing his big day with
money intended for the family's food; the maestro, more subtlely,
by his prolonged absences and an increasing recognition of his
own impotence.

"El cubilete" creates more tension than "Las conferencias."
Though one cannot really identify with Mario, the reader becomes
involved in the story because he knows something is going to

happen. From the moment of Don Leonardo's arrival, "excessively well-groomed, with the inevitable carnation in his buttonhole and his thin hair slicked back to perfection" (105), the air is charged with electricity. Everyone is aware of the Boss's arrival: "There was a scraping of chairs; everyone imperceptibly corrected his posture and sat up straighter in his chair" (105–6). Even though he is a most unattractive character, one may still feel some slight sympathy for Mario, for the childlike way he submits himself to the day's torture knowing that with each round of drinks he faces bitter humiliation. Then, as sometimes happens with a trusting child, his miracle happens; he bluffs out one more day. His luck is running. The closing paragraph (with its echoes of Ramón López Velarde's patriotic poem "Suave patria") depicts a man riding on the crest, a man at one with his world:

He threw the dice: threes. He picked them up and knew he would make his throw. He shook the dice cup, rattling the dice as one would a seed in the heart of a ripe fruit, and in the dry, hollow rumble he felt he was shaking mountains and beaches, fields and fish, mines, cattle, the entire fatherland of civics and geography lessons. He threw, and announced tranquilly:
"My pot, gentlemen."

II *Two Stories of Poverty*

Two of the stories in *La caja vacía* are about the *very* poor, the title story, and "Media docena de sábanas." The protagonist of the latter is a woman named Susana. Although Mexican, Susana, like the lecturer in "Las Conferencias," knows the sensation of being the outsider. Susana was wooed, and brought to Xalapa, by a husband who is not at all the man he represented himself to be. Now, several years later, she has three young children and a drunken husband to support. Susana copes with her problems by refusing to consider them. Weak from hunger, unable to feed her children, she lies in her filthy hut hour after hour, closing out the world. From time to time she tries to take in washing to earn a few *centavos*, but her work is so unsatisfactory that no one is willing to give her a job.
The specific action in "A Half-Dozen Sheets" concerns a last

opportunity that arrives in the form of a job no other woman will undertake, a bundle of fine wash for a woman no town washer-women will serve. The scorn of the other women means nothing to Susana, for she is already considered an outsider. From her advance, Susana prepares the first food she and the children have had in days. After dark, after she has washed the six sheets in the bundle of fine wash and spread them outside to dry, she hears her drunken husband stumbling home. He comes to her. He hears the remaining coins clinking in her pocket. They quarrel over the money. After a furious struggle her husband strikes her and walks away, shouting in rage.

It was then he became entangled in the sheet. Instinctively, without a thought, he took one lace corner in both hands and ripped the damned rag that seemed to be attacking him; the second, the third, the fourth, were intentional, rrrh, rrrrh, rrrrh, rrrrh, one after an-other, all six sheets. (48–49)

Neither attractive nor intelligent nor strong, not even crafty, Susana is entirely without defenses. She withdraws into slow and certain starvation. One knows there are many Susanas. It is not surprising that "Media docena de sábanas" has been translated into Russian.

"La caja vacía" is the story that Carballido expanded into the play *Silencio, pollos pelones, ya les van a echar su maíz.* The setting is a small community whose geographical situation is basic to the story line: it lies beside a dangerous river, with mountains on the other side. "Media docena de sábanas," "El cubilete," and "Las conferencias," are all simple stories, stories about a short period of time in the life of one central character. "La caja vacía" is much more complex. Only ten pages long, it is amazingly compact. There are two stories, really, which are brought together at the point where the lives of their characters intersect.

The plot of the major story line recounts the struggle for survival of a rural Mexican family. The head of the family, Porfirio, leaves to join other men who are collecting herbs to sell to two gringos. He is too impatient to wait for the funicular the gringos have rigged to ferry workers across the river. He attempts to swim across, but he misjudges the current and drowns. His body is washed downstream and cannot be found. His survivors, consisting only of women and children, are doubly bereft. They have lost the mainstay of the family, and worse, there is not even a body to mourn. While the gringos and the other men continue the search for Porfirio's body, the women realize they must seek help. There is no food, no money for a burial, not even a drop of coffee to offer the mourners. A neighbor tells them that the only thing to do is to go to Doña Leonela for help.

The story within the frame is that of Doña Leonela. For years Doña Leonela has devoted her time and her considerable fortune to her "Shelter of the Virgin Guadalupe." When her nephew becomes governor of the state he elevates her to the post of the chief of public assistance. But here she fails. Carballido describes the progression of frustration and disillusionment suffered by Doña Leonela, who is betrayed even by her beloved poor:

About the poor she finally learned the truth: they were beggars and fawners. There were so many of them, too many. By the end of the second year she despised them all. She tore up letters of recommendation without reading them; they were filthy; they were the ones responsible for the mountains of paperwork on her desk; they were trying to strip her of the last centavos of her budget. Oh, how she longed for the times of her "Shelter of the Virgin Guadalupe" when she could have had the pleasure of shoving them out and locking the door behind them, and with all the money she would have spent, buying a ticket to Europe and never returning. (12–13)

Doña Leonela refuses aid, but the assistant social worker listens to the pleas of Porfirio's mother and widow. She investigates the impoverished family. She attempts to impress Doña Leonelo with their very real need. Doña Leonela is adamant. As an expression of her sympathy the assistant sends the most luxurious coffin she can find.

At this point "La caja vacía" becomes both hilariously funny and extremely moving. The gift of a luxurious coffin to a family in need of food is ludicrous in the extreme. The coffin is too large to fit in their pitiful hovel. In the chicken house, it is befouled. Standing upright in the hut, it threatens to tip over and crush the occupants every time the train rumbles past. The problem of the empty coffin, for there still is no body to place in it, becomes grotesque. This family has more basic problems to face. But the last paragraph, again with macabre humor, offers a solution comprised of luck and invention.

Just as they were kneeling again [their neighbor] Doña Dalia began to cough, a racking cough that seemed to be her last. They waited until she again composed herself, and began to tell their beads. The widow and the mother were struck by the same idea, which they did not immediately communicate to one another. But surreptitiously they began to search the faces of everyone present, scrutinizing them for signs of exhaustion, or of age, or of illness. (16–17)

III   *Two Stories of Marital Relationships*

"La paz después del combate" was anthologized in the year's best Mexican stories in 1959 and in German translation in 1962. Structurally, the story is similar to "La caja vacía," that is, a frame story enclosing an interior sequence. In "La paz...," however, the internal story is a flashback that involves the characters of the frame, not different lives and different places. Another similarity is that both stories begin with the death of the head of a family. But in tone, "La paz después del combate" is more closely related to the remaining stories in *La caja vacía* than to the stories already discussed. Like them, it is more concerned with domestic relationships than with the world outside the home.

"La paz después del combate" concerns a love affair and a death. The death is untimely, and the love affair is scandalous. The present tense of the story spans only a few hours. It begins at dawn, beside the coffin of Adalberto. At eight o'clock flowers arrive. Shortly after eight comes a telephone call that is the story's inciting incident:

She hung up.
"Is Clementina coming?"
"Yes. And she's going to bring . . . Papa's first wife." (59)

As the widow, Marión, awakens, we are told in flashback of her first marriage, of Marión and Adalberto's meeting, and of their love affair. Once in the flashback, there is no further alternation between past and present until the interior story is completed. Marión and Adalberto run away, using the pretext of a medical conference being held in Vienna. Carballido recounts the complications, the snubs from friends, the frantic legal entanglements to be settled from their first marriages, and the gradual depletion of their funds. Marión bears Adalberto a daughter. The three are reduced to abject poverty.

Only two recourses remained: they had never planned to return to Veracruz, but that's where his consulting rooms were; or they could ask for help from the friends that had turned against them in Vienna. Marión chose to return home. That's how they returned to the field of battle. (67)

Carballido returns to the present with the words, "Marión drew her hair back into a bun. 'I look like the one who's dead,' she mused, and painted her cracked lips" (67).

Marión realizes that she no longer has any cause to do battle. Hatred has died with Adalberto. Without even hatred, she has *nothing* left. Marión and Adalberto's love was nourished because it was forbidden; it remained strong because of continuing opposition. The story ends with Marión's plea to a distant relative, a writer, to write the story of her love. With no husband, and no son—in a society which thinks of continuation of self through the figure of the first-born son, and Marión has borne only a daughter—Marión's hope for identity lies in the recreation of the meaning for her life. Only in the recording of the story, in a continuing circle of repetition, can she prevent dissolution.

In *La caja vacía* it would be difficult to find any male character worthy of emulation. Most, in fact, are not even sympathetic. At best, they are self-centered egotists; at worst, they are drunken bullies, and sadists. In the case of Miguel, the male figure in "Las flores blancas" (translated into Italian and included among the best short stories of 1966), there is little doubt. A sneak and a cheat, he is one of Carballido's most antipathetic characters.

Miguel's wife Adriana is the central figure of "Flores blancas."

Adriana's best friend Rosario has been living in Mexico, is divorced, and the women have not seen each other for a number of years. Adriana has spent days in preparation for Rosario's visit. She has filled Rosario's room with so many white blossoms that it resembles a bridal bower. (This is a touch of delicate irony that one remembers only after the beauty of the room has been defiled.)

Adriana, Miguel and their children meet Rosario at the train. Carballido carefully builds this story toward the irrevocable action that will change associations forever. The reunion is stiff and uncomfortable. Dinner is an uncomfortable interlude of empty chatter and false gaiety. A storm breaks as dessert is served. The lights go out. The children wake and Adriana asks Miguel to see about them. In the candlelight, alone at the table, the barriers of time and strangeness dissolve, and the two women begin to talk. Adriana reveals that weeks pass during which Miguel pays no attention to her. Miguel is involved with an ugly, unpleasant prostitute, not nearly as attractive as she. Rosario in turn confides that her loneliness, more than attraction, has involved her in a few brief affairs. The women look up to see Miguel standing listening in the doorway. Adriana feels her throat tighten. Miguel will never approve of Rosario. But Miguel says goodnight very naturally, and they all go to bed.

Adriana wakens in the night. She is aware that her husband is not lying beside her. She sits straight up in bed, no longer drowsy. She hears only the rain, and the beating of her pulse in her ears, and:

Suddenly she knew. . . . Rosario's startled surprise, the stealthy footsteps that stopped beside her bed; she could imagine every detail . . . unhappy, frightened Rosario, not daring to shout, vigorously trying to reject that stupid fool: "You'll wake Adriana, go away, get out of here"; . . . she wanted to cry, shout, but she didn't dare move. "She was fast asleep when I left her," the shadow murmured. She felt the cautious, but confident hand. . . . He lay down beside her, slowly, cautiously. . . . Don't be afraid, she's asleep." He put his arms around her, forced his tongue between her teeth. She could say nothing, dared not make a sound. Suddenly she imagined the wife lying awake and terrified, paralyzed like her, mute with horror. (101)

In a few striking final lines, Carballido underscores the irony of the purity and beauty of the fragrant white blossoms. The virginal air of the flower-banked room is a sad and ridiculous repudiation of unpleasant reality:

"Help me arrange them."
And they began to replace the vases, one after another, until the room was again inundated in white blossoms. The servant entered to tell them that breakfast was prepared. (102)

IV The Road From Youthful Illusion to Reality

"La desterrada," originally published in 1956, collected in *La caja vacía* in 1962, and anthologized in 1964, is dedicated to Carballido's mother. It might well be dedicated to all elderly persons nostalgic for old places and old ways. Equally important in the story is the grandson who travels his personal road to disillusion as he accompanies his grandmother on her voyage into her past.

Leonor, this lonely old woman now living in Mexico City, has tried to recreate the atmosphere of her youth by converting a sterile tenement balcony into verdant tropical growth. Lenor's devotion to her plants is paralleled in her devotion to her younger grandson. With the same devotion with which she tends the plants that remind her of her home, she nurtures the memory of her past in her grandson. Every night after they have watered the plants and she has helped him get ready for bed, she tells the child stories of her youth, of their scattered family, of the well and the huge mango tree, of life as it was lived in the hot country.

"La desterrada" recounts the disillusion that accompanies the grandmother's attempt to return home as well as the youth's distressing disappointment in the place he knows only through his grandmother's accounts. The disenchantment begins with the first sight of the river: "'Papaloapam means "river of butterflies,"' his grandmother told him" (124). But instead of "flowing blue waters, alive with the flashing color of great birds in flight," (124) the child sees only a turbid stream. There is a bus now, cheaper than the river launch, and the trip from the train is dusty and uncomfortable; where was the romantic journey downriver? The square, remembered by Leonor and imagined by the child, is empty and bare—the beautiful flowers, the fragrant orange trees, are all gone. By the time they reach the house, both are prepared for its ruinous condition. The house, the town, the hot country as Leonor knew them no longer exist. When she dies, these places and objects which were once a reality will fade a little more; they will die when the last memory that holds them dies.

The bitter awareness that she exists only in the present destroys Leonor. When she returns to Mexico City she can no longer believe her vision of the past. She is displaced in time as well as in space. She sells or gives away her flower pots, her lush ferns and tropical plants. There is no need to continue the illusion that she can *recreate a place that does not exist*. The place is no longer there, the meaning is no longer there. She thinks briefly of the memories she has implanted in her grandson. But memory is not real—reality is real. And an old woman's rejection of happy memory prematurely propels her grandson toward harsh reality.

The child in "Danza antigua" is named Palmira, the eldest of three girl children. Their father is dead. Their mother works to support her family, and their grandmother lives with them to look after them. Carballido's portrayal of the shifting emotions that change an old woman's devoted love for her favorite grandchild into anger and antagonism makes "Danza antigua" one of his most sensitive short stories.

Very simply, "Danza antigua" is a story about a before and an after. Palmira, once the favored, becomes the persecuted when she witnesses an act that shames her grandmother. The story begins after the embarrassing incident, told in flashback, and builds in tension to a scene in which a drunken Efraín—the grandmother's son, Palmira's uncle—beats the child with a belt. The grandmother watches with a glint of satisfaction in her eyes. Hilaria, Palmira's mother, finds out about the cruel whipping. Quietly and sadly she packs her mother's belongings and sends her to live with Efraín. That night Palmira grows up. The next day, from that time on, the responsibility for the house and for the care of the other children will be hers.

It can be said that "Danza antigua" is a story about a girl-child's becoming a woman. It is, but the corollary situation, the loss of childhood innocence, is more strongly emphasized.

It was during the days that her grandmother and she still loved each other very much. . . . Once the day's work was finished, the grandmother, alone and quiet in the little house, could pour herself a cup of coffee, and standing, slowly sipping her coffee, begin to remember. . . .
"How did that music go?"

One day Palmira interrupts her grandmother while she is dancing, petticoats held high. She laughs with childish pleasure, but is startled to hear her grandmother scream with anger: "She was still for an instant, and then rushed forward. She struck the child several times (she had never touched her before) and then fled into the patio, weeping loudly and accusing Palmira of having spied on her" (81). The old lady feels exposed and humiliated, and the child feels unjustly accused. The rift is irremediable. Before, Palmira was a child, and after, she is a woman. Again, two lives are saddened and changed by an old woman's excursion into the past.

In writing about the process of emerging from childhood, Carballido portrays a continuing series of disillusionments and losses. One leaves a world where light is filtered through rainbow mists to emerge in a harsh light that illuminates all too clearly the imperfection that has always been there.

Quique, in "Los prodijios," is very young to be exposed to the harsh and painful glare of loneliness and disillusion, but on the morning of the story he is forced to take a big step forward. On this day, he loses his faith in magic. Quique's day begins marvelously. He wakens and dresses himself without any help at all. He is full of his surprise, and runs to tell his aunt. Outside, in the sunshine, a figure stands pumping water. As he approaches, he sees a glorious sight: "An enormous arch, transparent, stripes of vivid colors higher than his aunt floated in the air, suspended in the mist surrounding the pump" (52). He can not hear his aunt's explanation for admiring "that fantastic, untouchable, transparent band through which he can see the glistening wall of flowering vines" (52).

The child wanders through the garden. Then he sees something that makes him stop short. He wants to touch, to tell, to
do something to celebrate the pure magic of the thing he sees,
a spider's web.

But a resplendent spider's web, of a perfect symmetry, woven
in the arbitrary, plushy architecture of the great geranium; each
thread seemed to correspond to a greater plan, each thread played
an astonishing geometrical game with all the other threads; it was
the net of an enchanted fisherman, it was a hammock of glass, and
upon each thread glittered many beads, like those on the rods of
the abacus on which he had still not learned to count, but these
were beads of glass, of water, and each carried within it hidden
fires that sparkled, each was a miniature star, a flashing jewel that
at any moment, ever so smoothly, might roll, or fall, for the entire
web vibrated and resonated visibly with the slightest breath of air.

It is his human impulse to reach out to another human that
causes him to overhear his aunts, that bursts his bubble of
happiness at the moment it is most resplendent:

"How long, then, are they going to leave him here with us?"
"Well, I don't know, my dear, indefinitely, I suppose, until the
poor thing finds some work, or can make some kind of living."
"And do you believe she'll be able to find a job?"
"How could that man abandon them like this."
"Well, Bibi, you see he did."
"Wouldn't you know, just when I really can't put up with
children any longer." (55–56)

A delicate and simple story, "Los prodijios" is another version
of the timeless theme of the loss of innocence in the garden.
Quique is exposed to the reality of evil in his world. He has
tasted the fruit of awareness and found it bitter. His gardens will
forever be less beautiful because of the knowledge of the presence of the serpent lurking there.

"Los huéspedes" is the longest of the short stories in *La caja
vacía*. In its structural complexity it is reminiscent of the title
story of the collection. It is probably not coincidental, then,
that these are the two stories Carballido has expanded into
plays. The family group of "Los huéspedes" appears in *La danza*

que sueña la tortuga and in *Un vals sin fin sobre el planeta*,
but it is *La danza* that most closely parallels the action of "Los
huéspedes."

In the preceding stories, the actions of adults have had adverse
effects upon the children they touch, almost as if the adults,
either from jealousy or from resentment caused by the harshness of their own lives, hope to make the children as unhappy as
they themselves are. Again, in "Los huéspedes," there is such an
attempt. But unlike the other children Carballido describes,
Carlos retains something of his delight in life and in people.

The "guests" are two young teenagers who come to the door
of the Moredia family to try to sell some jewelry in order to
reach their dying mother's bedside. The romance of their story
fascinates the family's innocents—Carlos and his two maiden
aunts, Aminta and Rocío. They are moved by the determination and love of the little brother and sister, and by their re-
sourcefulness and self-sacrifice in trying to obtain money for
their trip by selling their family gold. Guillermina, more cautious,
and less moved, waits for her husband Víctor to arrive home
before making any decision. The sympathetic and conspiratorial
threesome, the boy and the aunts, play on Víctor's pride. Convincing him of his magnaminity, they talk him into letting the
young people stay the night, into buying their train tickets, and
in addition, into giving them the price of the jewelry for their
expenses.

Carlos is mesmerized by the two, particularly by the girl.
She is like no one he has ever known, full of excitement and
laughter. She recites poetry, and constantly creates imaginary
scenes in which she is the center of attention.

It is only after they have waved goodbye at the train that
Carlos can see them clearly. And even when Guillermina tri-
umphantly proves that Consuelo was not the author of the
verses she claimed as her own, even after she attempts to dispel
the romance of their story—"You know what? They put one
over on us. They were running away together" (28)—Carlos is
not disillusioned. Guillermina does not mar his impression of
Consuelo and Gabriel. For a brief instant, Carlos shared their
unrestrained excitement and freedom. They have become an
unforgettable moment in his life, in dream and in reality.

In contrast to Carballido's dramatic writing, and except for "La caja vacía," there is no humor in this group of short stories. One finds themes of social importance, as in "La caja vacía" and "Media docena de sábanas," but these are themes more fully developed in the plays. Neither does one find the experimentation, the variety of form and technique, notable in his dramatic works.

Instead, *La caja vacía* is an often-poetic, usually nostalgic, homogeneous group of mood pieces. Details of place and custom are perceptive and evocative. These are clear, simple, quiet stories portraying of a way of life in a southern province of Mexico.

CHAPTER 4

The Longer Prose Fiction

CARBALLIDO has published four works that in Spanish are classified as novels: *La veleta oxidada, El norte, Las Visitaciones del diablo*, and *El sol*. Of the four, only *Las Visitaciones* approximates traditional English-language novel length. It is often difficult to define the line that separates the short novel from the long short story, and by the single application of length, the three briefer pieces could possibly be classified as long short stories. This distinction is particularly difficult in the case of Carballido's first novel, *La veleta oxidada*. But by the addition of the criterion of conceptual and stylistic complexity, *La veleta oxidada*, as well as *El norte* and *El sol*, are clearly novellas, rather than long short stories. In each there are a number of important characters. There are more frequent and complex shifts in time and setting than is usual in the short story. Even more important, there is considerable depth of psychological development. These novellas are characterized by depth and breadth, as well as linear progression, a richness and fullness that is a proper hallmark of the novelistic tradition.

I La veleta oxidada

La veleta oxidada[1] was published in 1956. It is the story of an artistically ambitious woman who is married to a man who is basically decent, but totally devoid of interest in the arts. (This theme, incidentally, appears again four years later in Carballido's play *Las estatuas de marfil*.) The provincial setting, and the absence of intellectual stimulation more common in a city, are essential to the novella.

The novel's protagonist is Martha Cruz Roca, the wife of Adán Luna, a provincial landowner whom she met while both

69

were students in Mexico City. Adán's widowed sister Adela lives with them. Martha is the outsider; she misses the stimulation of her university days. A member of a local literary club, she feels intellectually superior to the other members. In her home, too, she is unable to adapt comfortably, because her sister-in-law Adela frequently usurps the authority Martha believes should be hers as Adán's wife. Martha's increasing dissatisfaction with her life precipitates the events of *La veleta oxidada*.

One must emphasize the simplicity of style of this novella. Chapters are often only several pages long, and characterization and action are handled in succinct fashion. Carballido has said that "the first" half of the novel is "a kind of shorthand version of a fuller novel," though as it progresses, "the novelistic rhythm improves."[2] But even when one is aware of its deficiencies, one wonders that Carballido can convey so much and present such wholly formed characters in such a brief space.

In the early chapters, three significant events occur. The first is the arrival of Nieves, a servant girl, to the household. With typical Carballido economy of scene, even the *event* of her arrival is important, as it affords Martha an opportunity to overhear gossip about her personal life. Nieves's mother pleads with Adela to take good care of Nieves:

"Don't wish that job on me. I can't be responsible for her."
"But at least here in your house. . . ."
"And what could happen here?"
"Well, there's Adancito . . . I wouldn't want her. . . ."
"Oh, Adán. He hasn't even got his wife pregnant. . . . Didn't you know they don't sleep together?" (14–15)

This exchange infuriates Martha, and it is one of two specific events that cause her to reconsider the course her life is following.

The second event is a disastrous gathering of her literary group. Martha is more than usually irritated by the artistic ineptitude of her guests. She criticizes them openly, and becomes infected with the sense of her own mischief. Adán arrives toward the end of the evening, drunk. Without greeting any of his wife's guests, Adán turns off the record player and goes to his room. The guests are dismayed, doubly so when Martha abruptly bids them good evening. When her guests react with sympathy, it merely adds to her fury.

"Of course, Martha dear, we all understand."
"Understand what?" A harsh, insolent voice they'd never heard before.
They went out to the street. It had rained and the paving stones shone wetly. The doorway framed Martha's mocking smile. As Lolita turned to say something, she stumbled on the sidewalk and fell. Martha laughed uproariously and softly closed the door. Then she went to her room and fell facedown on her bed, sobbing. (48)

There is a third event in these first brief chapters that until the end of the novella seems peripheral to Martha's life. The cook's three-year-old son dies, and Adela gives permission for the wake to be held in the Luna home. Martha is shocked by the barbarity of the preparations for the wake. The cook dresses the child in white, makes up his face with cosmetics obtained from the servant Nieves's sister, who works in a brothel, and then hires a photographer to take his picture. During the wake, as the funeral rockets rise against the sky, a strange image occurs to Martha. "The rockets were helping the soul of the little angel in its painful and stumbling ascent toward Heaven. . . . Sssssss boom! And he was helped a little further" (34–35).
Not because of the funeral, of course, but as a result of the gossip about her not being pregnant, and her quarrel with her "intellectual" friends, Martha decides to go to Mexico City, with Adán, for corrective surgery.
The interval there reveals a great deal about chances for communication between Martha and Adán. Martha is in her glory. She writes a poem about her operation, and then an accompanying commentary about the poem that is more widely read than the poem itself. Adán, on the other hand, is as bored and restless as Martha had been in the provinces. It is clear that the couple share few spiritual interests. Following the operation, there is a temporary improvement in their marriage. They recreate the days of their courtship, visiting familiar

scenes and playing at being sweethearts. The idyll comes to an
end when Adán wants to make love to Martha. Her insistence
that it will be harmful to her, and his persistence, causes a
quarrel that breaks their relationship anew. Adán plans to return home and leave Martha in the city to follow when she
feels like rejoining him. Grateful for her reprieve Martha allows
Adán to make love to her.

Midpoint in the novella the characters of three of the principal
figures are clearly delineated. Adán is a man who aspires to
little beyond the simple pleasures afforded him as a provincial
landowner. Martha is seen as frustrated and intellectually shallow
(in spite of her own evaluations), an immature woman who
would rather be a sweetheart to her husband than a wife. Adela
is the provincial widow who worships her brother and scorns the
educated and liberated woman he chose to marry. The accord
that might have been achieved by Martha's desire to become
a mother is dissipated by her resistance to becoming a traditional
provincial wife.

It is when Adán returns alone from Mexico City that Nieves
—inevitably, predictably—becomes the fourth important figure in
the novella. Adán, angered and injured by Martha's rejection,
turns to this young, admiring, and complaisant girl. Then, three
months after she and Adán parted in Mexico City, Martha comes
hurrying home to announce the much-desired pregnancy. She
does not receive the reaction she had hoped for. Adán is surprised, but unmoved. Because of Martha's long absence, Adela,
and the group Martha had formerly considered her friends,
speculate maliciously upon the child's parentage.

Now, three fourths of the way through this novella, the pace,
which had been quiet, almost static, changes. Martha discovers
that Nieves, in the same stages of pregnancy as Martha, is also
carrying Adán's child. This revelation initiates a chain of actions
that become almost visual. Nieves is dismissed. She goes to her
sister, who is still with La Flaca. Adán learns where Nieves is.
He pays the sister's debts and takes both girls, all of them on
horseback, up a steep mountain trail to a mountain farm.
Martha learns where Adán is. She, too, rides up the trail where
she confronts Adán; she confesses that her literary aspirations
have been largely spurious, and asks his forgiveness.

Adán watched her cry. He handed her a handkerchief. He didn't
dare touch her until he'd spoken first. How should he tell her? It
was all so much simpler than she thought, what the hell. . . . Finally
he said:
"Look."
She looked at him, anxious. "Yes, Adán."
"Look . . . ," and burst out: "There's nothing for us to talk over,
we just don't like to sleep together anymore!" And lowering his voice,
"And I don't like it in town." (88)

But the line of physical action is not quite complete. Martha
rides back down the mountain. Her child is born, dead. Now it is
the end of journeys.

The stillborn child is the image of the Luna family, obviously
Adán's child. The community is moved by Martha's suffering.
She is one of them now, while Adán, the native, has become
the outcast. Adela must revise her opinion of Martha and shift
her position to align herself with Martha and against Adán.
And in final emphasis of reversals of stance, there is the burial
of Martha and Adán's child:

They wanted to bury the child in the morning, but Martha
refused: she had clothing bought, and a tiny cape; she propped
the little body on the table and called in the photographer.

Weeping, in physical pain, barely able to move, she arranged the
flowers, following the advice of the cook, who was also weeping
copiously. "Yes, that's how it should be. I want everyone to see him."
(92)

That night rockets filled the sky, as Martha thought: "The dark
little doll, dressed in white, was wandering around up there
through the desolation of the zodiac and planets, seeking his
way, some sign of his road. . . . Sssss boom! And another rocket
came to assist him in his ascent . . ." (92).

Each of the novella's principal characters has turned in the
winds of fate. Each has assumed a new, and rigid, course,
fixed for some time to come, even though it may be set dead
against the wind. When Adela asks Martha, "And when can we
bury him?" Martha replies: "Not until he rots." And with the
last chapter, all movement ceases, situations become static, the
weathervane rusts into place.

Carballido makes dramatic use of pace in *La veleta oxidada,* the contrast between the unhurried, repetitious way of life in the first three quarters of the book and the strong sense of physical movement in the last five chapters. The style is simple and clear, reading like a schema for a work that will later be amplified. And as is typical of Carballido's prose fiction, there is very little description of place. The emphasis is on character, on human relationships, on the marble that hits another that glances off another that strikes the original marble; these are the important elements in *La veleta oxidada,* as they will be in his next novella, *The Norther.*

II   *From a Stationary Weathervane to the Winds of a Norther*

Carballido's second novella, published in 1958, only two years after *La veleta oxidada,* is his most widely distributed work of prose fiction, republished in Venezuela in 1967, translated into English in 1968, and included in *10 novelas latinoamericanas* in 1970. *El norte*[3] is a much more developed and sophisticated novella than *La veleta oxidada,* and structurally, one of Carballido's most interesting works. The book consists of fifteen chapters. The odd-numbered chapters, one through fifteen, are the present tense of the novella. They move in chronological progression and recount events that are happening *now.* The even-numbered chapters, two through fourteen, are flashback sequences. They, too, move in chronological order, and they describe events that exist only in the characters' memories. These chapters are the past tense of the novella.

There are three major characters in *El norte*: Isabel, Aristeo, and Max. The odd chapters (the present) take place in a port town in the state of Veracruz. The setting for the even-numbered chapters is apparently Mexico City. Max appears only in present time, Aristeo and Isabel in both.

In the opening chapter the reader is introduced to Aristeo and Isabel, who are on holiday. The day of their arrival the weather is beautiful, but the very first night a cold, persistent fog settles over the town, carried by the norther of the title. Aristeo and Isabel are registered in their boardinghouse as aunt and nephew, a relationship chosen because of the wide disparity in their ages. Even so, it is clear to everyone that they are lovers.

The background situation, revealed in the alternate, even-numbered chapters, is fairly simple. Isabel is a widow. By Aristeo's standards, at least, she is well-to-do. Isabel had been married by her family to a man many years her elder who through accident, more than by design, introduced her to the delights of sex. Once a widow, she retreated into an existence from which she escaped through the illusory world of movies. Aristeo, from a very poor family, was an usher at one of the theaters Isabel frequented. One evening he rescued Isabel from a drunk who had hidden in the ladies' room. At her invitation, Aristeo visited Isabel's home to accept payment for her gratitude. This encounter initiated an affair that became increasingly comfortable for both.

Isabel has periods when she questions an involvement with a man so much younger than she, but her desire to be with Aristeo is much stronger than her conscience. Aristeo's only reservation about their affair is that Isabel is often the aggressor in their lovemaking. Shaming him, even hurting him physically, seems to whet her sexual appetite. But because he respects her, he is unable to parry her attacks. Actually, Aristeo is so pleased to be pampered and supported financially that he accepts the drawbacks in the arrangement. And, too, he is genuinely fond of Isabel.

In the past tense of the novella Aristeo and Isabel's relationship begins with a seduction. In the half of the book dealing with the present their relationship *ends* with a seduction. Full circle—the story of an affair.

The third principal figure, Max, is an intruder. He is a drifter, aimless, purposeless, purely existential—a catalyst who precipitates crises without being touched himself. His ethical code is completely foreign to Isabel's (and many readers') middle-class standards. To some degree he seems unreal; he is quite real enough, however, to disrupt the balance of a satisfactory relationship—satisfactory, even if of doubtful permanence.

Aristeo meets Max at night, at a lighthouse. It is Max who opens the conversation. He realizes that Aristeo is fascinated by the boats, and invites him to come the next morning to inspect the sailing vessel on which he had arrived. Aristeo is too inept and too insecure to ask Isabel for the free time to go by himself

to Max's boat. He is surprised when Max shows up later to
join them on the beach. Max has allowed the boat to leave
without him, his only apparent motivation his new interest in
Aristeo. Isabel is offended by Max's assumption that he, Aristeo,
and Isabel are now a threesome. Max intrudes upon their routine
activities and contrives new ones for all three.

Then Max suggests to Aristeo that they sign on a freighter
bound for Havana. In their discussion Aristeo articulates for the
first time his feeling for Isabel:

"It's just that she's been a good old girl, I swear. And . . . well,
she's always been a good old girl."
"Who else does she go with? Isn't she married?"
"No. She doesn't have anyone. Just me." It filled him with pride
to say it, for the first time, and it added a new value to Isabel.
"She's a widow." (76)

Even so, the appeal of adventure and of Max's companionship
attracts Aristeo very strongly. His indecision costs him his
relationship with Isabel. Max drops by the next morning. He
finds Isabel alone. For no discernible reason, Max and Isabel
make love. They drift into it the way Max drifts into everything.
Isabel suffers remorse, but as Max explains it to Aristeo, it is
obvious that the experience had no effect, either negative or
positive, on him:

"So what happened?"—Max.
"About what? Oh, about Havana? I don't know."
"No, about Isabel."
"What *about* Isabel?"
"Did she tell you?"
"Did she tell me what?" He was prepared now.
"It wasn't my fault, or hers. . . . I went to look for you, and she
was getting up, in her dressing gown. . . ."
"Don't tell her I told you." Another silence. "Listen, the boat
leaves tomorrow." (94–95)

Aristeo is not so stolid. Hurt more than he would have believed
possible, he punches Max on the jaw—and he breaks his relationship with Isabel.

As the novella ends Aristeo is alone, walking along the shore toward the lighthouse that holds such fascination for him:

He thought he heard a sound that corresponded to the light of the beacon; he listened to it; more than imagining it, he listened with his skin, with his stomach. A long, piercing note, as from a high-speed saw, for the circular track, and a little crystal bell for the spark. He tried to make the sound with his mouth; no, that wasn't it. He looked, and listened to it, again. A great wave broke over him and he yelled. He stood rooted there, streaming water, shouting and laughing; he wiped his wet hair from his eyes, pounded his drenched body, licked the salt from his lips. Never had he been so alone. He was at the brink of perceiving something that was not yet clear; rather, he desired it intensely. . . . He was aware only of his own soaked body, of the tossing of the sea, of the colors of the sky, of the icy water. He was himself, master of himself, his mouth and eyes smarting from the salt.

He began to run, jumping over pools of water, toward the light-house. (100)

There are two circular lines of movement in *El norte*, one within the other. The larger circle is Isabel's line. It encompasses the span of the book, beginning with a seduction, ending with a seduction. The inner circle relates to Aristeo, beginning at the lighthouse with his first tentative steps alone, and ending at the lighthouse, when he is completely alone. Max is merely a tangential figure whose line interrupts the circles from time to time. For Isabel, the events in the book mark a beginning and an end. For Aristeo, they are an introduction, a beginning. Max has neither beginning nor end. He is as near the essence of freedom as a human being can be.

The ending is open to interpretation. Aristeo's feeling of being completely alone, the fact he is running toward the compellingly hypnotic eye of the lighthouse, might be interpreted as a race toward oblivion. His fascination with Max, and a possible Freudian interpretation of the lighthouse as a classic phallic symbol, might suggest a future for Aristeo diametrically opposed to his past. Most convincing is that the multiplicity of sensations Aristeo is experiencing—cold, wetness, sound, the taste of salt in his mouth and the stinging of salt

in his eyes—indicate an acute awareness of life. The realization
that he is more alone than he has ever been is a man's realization, not a boy's. *El norte*, then, is a classic novel of initiation—
and, not to forget Isabel, the story of a woman's growing old.

III A Novel of Suspense and Romance:
Las visitaciones del diablo

Carbadillo's third, and longest work of prose fiction was
published in 1965. *Las visitaciones del diablo*,[4] like the earlier
El norte, is divided into fifteen sections. There is no further
similarity between the two, however, either in concept or in
effect. *Las visitaciones del diablo* bears the subtitle, *folletín
romántico en XV partes*. Its chapters, therefore, are more than
usually emphatic divisions. They are episodic, consciously
modeled in the manner of romantic serials—adventure by
installment.

It is difficult to decide in this novel whether Paloma or
Lisardo is the more important figure. Either might be the
protagonist. There is no confusion about the setting, it is
essential to the story. The Estrella family home provides an
effective gothic setting. It is musty and dark, near the edge
of a river, with passageways and garden walks that create a
suitably mysterious background for the visitations of the devil.

Arminda and Felix Estrella are the parents of a romantically
beautiful daughter, Angela. Angela is bedfast, the result of a
fall, and two subsequent, and disastrous, operations. These three
form the nucleus of the Estrella houschold. Lisardo, an
Estrella cousin, becomes the fourth member when he arrives
following five years of schooling and travel abroad. This education has in large part been financed by his uncle Félix, his
father's brother. Lisardo then, and Angela are first cousins. A
step down the scale socially, halfway between the family and the
servants, there is Toña, who had been wet nurse first to
Arminda, and then to Arminda's daughter Angela. Paloma, the
female protagonist, is Toña's granddaughter. Paloma becomes
part of the Estrella household when her father dies and she
comes to live with her grandmother. Paloma's arrival is the first
incident of the book. There are several unnamed servants, and

three who are of some importance to the story: Eulalia, Egas, and Juan.

Carballido purposefully and carefully develops an air of mystery and suspense in *Las visitaciones,* but he also makes a number of things clear from the beginning. For example, Paloma does not fit into her niche as a quasi-servant in the house. Her father was a schoolteacher. From him she learned more than academic subjects. She is proud, sophisticated, and intellectually superior to Arminda, Félix, and Angela. She is resentfully aware of the ambiguity of her position, which is, essentially, that of unpaid companion to Angela. It is also clear from the beginning that Félix and Arminda are extremely ambitious socially, and that they dote upon their daughter Angela. They have no doubt that Lisardo would be a fine match for Angela, and they believe it would be only just for him to discharge his obligation to them by accepting the responsibility for their beautiful, but crippled, daughter. The fact that Carballido makes most apparent is that there are strong undercurrents in the Estrella household.

The mystery and suspense in the book center about the nocturnal visits of the devil. Basically the reader feels that these occurrences are not supernatural, although he soon becomes aware that there *is* a devil, or perhaps more than one devil, within the house. The reader's natural desire to identify this spirit is facilitated by increasing indications that it is female. Since the point of view of the narration is often Lisardo's, the fact that he witnesses two of the appearances eliminates him as a possible suspect, even were the figure not female. Félix, too, is eliminated; in addition, he is too uncomplicated to be involved in any activity requiring subterfuge. His night visitations have a more straightforward purpose—the servant Eulalia is considerably more voluptuous than his wife.

It is from the distaff members of the household that the reader must identify the devil figure: Eulalia, Egas, Toña, Arminda, Angela, or Paloma. Any of these six could have been responsible for the first appearance of the devil. (The experienced reader of suspense will not eliminate Angela as a suspect, even though she is apparently paralyzed, and carried everywhere by the strong, silent servant, Juan.) Carballido sets the stage for the first visit.

Again the insomnia. It was a while before Lisardo decided to open
the book. . . . He read: "*Interesting and Curious Recollections of an
Estate in China*," by B. H. Then: . . . Quietly he slipped down the
hall and peered cautiously through the window. He saw a horrifying
demon with a green face and sharp, saw-pointed teeth; he was
stretching a human skin over the bed, painting it with an artist's
brush. Then the demon threw the brush aside, and shaking the skin,
as one would an overcoat, he threw the skin over his shoulders and
became the girl! (37–38)

It is late that evening, after Lisardo had read about this
supernatural event, that the devil makes its first appearance:

Then he heard a sound, as if someone were trying to get in.
Were they pushing the door? The sound ceased. . . . It began
again. . . . There was no one there. . . . Then suddenly he felt the
presence, and out of the corner of his eye he glimpsed a white
shape that immediately pressed itself against his body, someone or
something that clutched him in a heated embrace . . . he felt a
feminine warmth and pressure, and a hand touched his chest and
caressed it, and slipped down to his belly and caressed it, and
slipped lower, stroking and caressing. (38–39)

The first visitation is sexual, the "devil" might be any of
the women of the household. The second visitation *seems* to
eliminate the crippled Angela, since it is she who is the victim
of the attack:

Lisardo bent over her.
"Angela, what happened?"
They helped her sit up; her face was covered with dirt, and her
cheek bore the mark of a blow.
"It hit me, and dragged me, dragged me, hit me," Angela sobbed.
Moaning, she ran her hands through her hair, and a loose strand
caught in her fingers, as if torn out by force. (81)

The seasoned reader of suspense will not have eliminated
Angela, however, for she might have engineered the attack
upon herself.
The third appearance of the devil is also directed against
Angela. Some cakes Lisardo has brought her from a gala evening

are poisoned. Angela is more frightened than harmed by the incident.

> The hair on his body stood on end from the contagion of the blind, uncontrolled horror demonstrated by Angela. He took her arms and shook her.
> "But, tell me, what was it? Tell me what it was!"
> "Poison, the little cakes. Poison."
> Then Lisardo noticed that the rose he had brought her was no longer on the bureau. He found it, crushed, on the floor. The neat squares of the little cakes were darkened by a heavy, molasseslike substance, and to one side, empty, stopperless, he found the vial of laudanum. (109)

Was the visit finally an indication of real danger for Angela, or the maneuver of a neurotic child motivated by frustration at having to miss the party?

The last attack—the reader has come to think of the visitations as attacks—is upon Paloma. Up to this point Paloma has seemed a prime suspect. She is disgruntled with her position in the Estrella house. She envies the attention Angela receives from Lisardo. However, Paloma is attacked in full view of Lisardo, and on this "visitation," which takes place by the riverbank, the devil is apprehended.

> The white figure moved toward her slowly, deliberately. Paloma had noticed nothing, and the white figure stood motionless. Then he watched it advance, as if the ground itself were sliding forward toward the riverbank. He could do nothing, it had already reached Paloma, and now Paloma had sensed it, was standing, was stepping backward; the white figure leapt upon her.
> "Angela, no!" (152)

Lisardo, and probably the reader, have reached the conclusion that it is Angela who is responsible for all the evil in the house.

> Lisardo ran toward them and grabbed their clothing; as he tugged, he shouted, for although the river was not deep, the rocks, the shadows, and the current lent a fictitious air of mortal danger to that riverbank that was crumbling away beneath the three of them. Half-fallen into the water, they clung to each other, the rocks were

rolling beneath them; it was unreal, chaotic. Then Paloma helped
him drag that whimpering bundle from the water. Blood trickled
down Paloma's face, she had injured her head on a sharp rock;
the three of them were streaming water. Arminda, clutching Lisardo's
leg, was shouting, shouting . . . something unintelligible. (153)

So the evil flows from Arminda, shallow, frustrated Arminda,
who is jealous of her own daughter, jealous of Lisardo's
attention to her, and resentful of the obligation to care for
Angela which keeps her tied to this provincial setting. When
Lisardo becomes disenchanted with Angela and turns to Paloma,
then Paloma becomes the target for Arminda's poisonous wrath.

The physical action of *Las visitaciones del diablo* comprises
the frame of a traditional suspense story. Carballido has also
created a typical nineteenth-century romantic novel. The pale,
languishing, paralyzed, blond beauty attracts the handsome,
sophisticated young man recently returned from Europe. Every
opportunity is given them to develop their love. The parents of
the young beauty offer wealth, ease, and social position in
return for the care of their beloved child. A silent male servant
carries the young girl, dressed in billowing and becoming gowns,
to the gardens where she waits for the young hero to come to
read to her. Only the reader/observer—and the true heroine,
the beautiful but lowly Paloma—can see the worm at the heart
of the apple. The hero, apparently, is blind to reality. He agrees
to marry Angela, and he and his fiancée's father toast the
future in fine old brandy in the dusty wine cellar, a cave deep
beneath the sprawling house.

But just in time the hero is saved from an irreparable mistake. He surprises his love reading one of the many pornographic
books that line the top shelves of her father's library. So she
can walk? His eyes are opened. Angela realizes she has lost
everything. She drops her mask, and Lisardo sees her as she really
is. Aware at last, he realizes Paloma's true worth and they run
away together, fleeing the evil of the house.

This plane in *Las visitaciones*, the story line following the
romantic tradition, is true to the genre. Carballido describes
ladies' shopping excursions and social visits, the obligatory gala,
and quiet hideaways for romantic trysts. All these elements

produce a very real picture of a vanished way of life, the indolent, easy life of a provincial upper-class nineteenth-century family. On the one hand, we have the romantic feuilleton promised by the subtitle. On the other, a novel of suspense in which an accomplished craftsman builds to an ending that is a surprise, but perhaps predictable to a reader astute enough to perceive the psychological clues given him along the way. (Carballido is so sure of his craft, for example, that he allows Arminda, the nightwalking evil spirit, to sing Bellini's "La sonámbula" at a musical evening halfway through the novel.)

But there is also a third plane in *Las visitaciones*, one based primarily upon characterization. And this third dimension is what makes the novel something more than a superficial mystery-romance. Carballido has produced complex, living characters that stand out in plastic reality from their two-dimensional background. As in several of his plays, it seems that Carballido enjoys the challenge of an exercise in ingenuity, the creation of something contemporary, something valid, within the mold of a stereotyped form.

Félix, the father, is fairly simple: he is materialistic and mildly lecherous; he is a real person, ready to drive a bargain to provide for his daughter's future. He is willing to capitalize on Lisardo's gratitude for past financial aid to seal that bargain. Arminda, Félix's wife, is more complex, one of the best drawn characters of the novel. She is torn between the necessity of staying at home with her crippled daughter, keeping up the appearance of being a conscientious mother, and her driving desire for social success. When Lisardo arrives her emotions are further complicated. She does desire her daughter's happiness, she wants to see her happily married, with her future assured. At the same time, her own need for romance is strong. She is married to a man who no longer desires her, and she is growing old. Her passions are intensified by the limited chances they have for realization. She is an example of one of Carballido's most prevalent themes: the wasted life. Waste *is* evil, and Arminda is so filled with evil that it must escape in the form of destructive impulses. There is a devil in the house, but it is the evil of unfilled life.

The three young people—Paloma, Lisardo, and Angela—have

interesting contradictions in both their personalities and their relationships. Lisardo is a strange hero. Attractive, but not heroic, he comes to the important decisions in his life by *not* acting; he follows the line of least resistance, and once he is involved in a course of action he follows that course. He makes no plans, and he has no particular expectations. He exists in the present.

Angela is a fairly standard character, devious and deceitful, and she is also reasonably predictable. She is a beautiful girl whose twisted leg so mars her own vision of herself that she prefers to feign total incapacity rather than walk in less than perfect grace. She is unable to transcend her limitations.

Paloma is the more interesting of the girls. She is the member of the Estrella group who is least similar to the others. She moves at the edge of their activities, silent, supercilious, contemptuous of their foibles. She is aware that Angela can walk. She wants Lisardo for herself, but her pride in her own superiority will not permit her to intervene in the course of Lisardo and Angela's love affair. Yet when Lisardo turns to her after his sorrowful renunciation of Angela ("I believe I am suffering greatly" [142]), she is warm, generous, and understanding:

> And he wept in Paloma's arms. Later, they kissed. Paloma's eyes were also damp, but for some reason of her own. They kissed. They clung to each other desperately: "Children lost in the woods, Hansel and Gretel," she thought. "I don't want to be alone tonight," he thought.
> They held each other so tightly they could barely climb the stairs.
> He locked the door of his room with difficulty, still holding Paloma tightly, as if he were afraid she would escape from him.
> Still kissing, mouth to mouth, they began to remove their clothes.

What lifts *Las visitaciones* to a new plane are the delightful ambiguities revealed at the end of the novel, ambiguities lying beneath the surface throughout the novel that Carballido reveals with a fine flourish of his cape. Listen to the grandmother:

> "Are you leaving us, lad?"
> "With your granddaughter."

"Don't call *her* my granddaughter . . . How can you leave my Angelita? What will she say." (157)

Hear the "hero": " 'Paloma must be waiting in the garden.' But he didn't want to see her. 'I don't love her. She's the same to me as any other' " (151). And the "heroine," in response to Lisardo's rather rueful observation that they are going to be very poor, reassures him with the announcement that she has stolen thirty-five hundred pesos from Félix's desk. In response to his astonishment and shock, she explains: " 'It's very little for my grandmother's life, for the milk she stinted her own children. And for the salary they never paid me' " (163).

What the reader has been following as a suspense/romance ends with an unconventional Paloma and Lisardo on a train to "somewhere," as Lisardo sings a phrase from the *Canzona di Bacco*: "Let he who would be happy, be so;/There is no certainty in tomorrow."[5]

IV *Return to Metaphor:* El Sol

In much the same way the rose is used as a metaphor in "Yo también hablo de la rosa," the sun, in the novella of the same name, is a metaphor for the process of becoming aware, or achieving knowledge—also parallel to the process of maturation. The novella begins and ends with the words "The sun," and most of the revelatory passages involve the sun: "But when he opens his eyes, when he sees: it's like blood. Something is happening in the sky, movement. There it is in front of him . . . almost: something rising. An image slipping from the shadows. When it emerges it will be horrible" (120).[6] (Although he shares a similar experience, "he was at the brink of discovering something that was not yet clear," Aristeo, in *El norte* [101], has a very different reaction: he is filled with joy.)

Essentially, *El sol* is the portrayal of a young boy's initiation into love, into manhood, and into pain. As in the short story "Los prodigios," the transition from childhood into the world of adults is tantamount to disillusion. A line from the closing paragraph of *El sol* makes this eminently clear: "Knowing is a horrendous compromise" (121).

This most recent of Carballido's major works of prose fiction

is divided into seven quite brief sections of from ten to fifteen
pages each. The first section serves primarily as introduction to
the characters: the reader meets Mario Escudero, the protagonist, and his older and wiser (perhaps "already initiated")
brother. Mario and Ricardo live in Mexico City, but have come
to a small village to spend their vacation with provincial
relatives, Juana, Celia, and Jorge. ("Celia ... seems the oldest
of the three; she is Juana's sister, but he calls her 'aunt,' because
she is the wife of Jorge, his father's uncle, his great-great uncle,
if that means anything. And Juana is just plain Juana" [20].)

There is a young and pretty servant girl named Hortensia in
the household. Not surprisingly, Mario—the right time, the
right place—falls in love with Hortensia. He is perplexed by
his combined feelings of incipient lust and romantic respect for
the girl. He wants to know all about love and women, but when
Ricardo offers rather graphic recitals of his own experiences,
Mario is strangely bothered by his brother's knowing explanations. Hortensia's sister Liboria, and Liboria's husband Efraín,
are the remaining characters in *El sol*.

As the novel progresses Carballido elaborates on young Mario's
feelings of love for Hortensia, his tentative, groping approaches
to her, his gift to her of a silver heart, and the experiencing
of these emotions in a new awareness and awe of nature. Mario
walks through the pinewoods on the mountains above the village,
attempting to come to terms with his surging emotions. The
leitmotiv "and the village below" is echoed throughout the
novel as Mario lies in *the sun* in the clear, pine-scented air,
pondering the meaning of love, indeed, of all the world around
him.

Celia become uncomfortably aware of her nephew Mario's
infatuation with the attractive young girl and she asks Liboria
to take her sister home with her. Mario is bereft, his adolescent
passions exacerbated by Hortensia's absence. He meets Hortensia
accidentally in the market. His elation at seeing her, and the
thrill he receives from a furtive embrace, are tempered by
Hortensia's insistent pleas that he convince his parents to take
her as a servant. He daydreams about the opportunities this
will present him to be alone with Hortensia. Then "romance"
conquers sex, and he is scandalized by his own imaginings.

Mario, in Hortensia's absence, becomes indolent and moody. He no longer wanders through the mountains. Instead, it is Ricardo who has become the explorer, absent for long hours. One night Ricardo returns from one of his nocturnal outings wet and whitelipped. He explains that he has slipped and fallen into the lake.

In the fifth section the tempo of *El sol* visibly increases. Liboria brings Hortensia back to Celia (and Mario), explaining that she cannot afford to keep her in her home. Hortensia seems strangely preoccupied, and spends much of her time compulsively washing her hair. Mario is still incapable of coping with his conflicting emotions, and he is especially troubled by this "new" Hortensia.

A week later, Efraín's body is found in the lake. Liboria, none too pleased with Efraín while he was living, is prostrate with grief. She will not allow Hortensia to stay with her. Hortensia refuses to go to the funeral with the family. Mario can sense the "black wave of suffering" issuing from the room Hortensia occupies behind the little store operated by the elderly aunts and uncle.

Ricardo, too, seems changed. He is drinking every night in the room that he and Mario share. His favorite leather jacket is stained, and he buys a chemical in the market to try to clean it. Hortensia is growing thin, and one day—to Mario's horror—she cuts off all her hair. Long before their vacation has ended, Ricardo proposes to Mario that they return home. Mario agrees to accompany his brother, but at the last moment, actually as the bus pulls out of the station, he cannot go; he senses that his brother is deeply troubled and he wants to help him, but he also feels the overwhelming pull of Hortensia's attraction. He stays. Late that evening he goes to Hortensia's room. He receives an unexpected welcome: "Take off your clothes," said a strange Hortensia. "I want you to tell me everything," Mario replies (108), and as Hortensia begins her story, the plot unravels.

The seventh and last section of the novel is told through Mario's consciousness as he waits for the bus to come to take him away from the village, during the bus ride, and during a blurred period of time after he has stopped the bus and run into the hills. These pages narrate the painful coming-to-terms with the knowledge of all that has happened—knowledge of deception and betrayal and murder. They are told in flashback—Hortensia's confession—and first-person stream of consciousness—Mario's ordering of all the information now in his possession.

Since the reader has seen all the events of the novella through Mario's eyes (not always in first-person narrative, but always from his point-of-view), many of the important events of the novel have taken place outside his "view"—a fact that is quite fitting given Mario's innocence and naiveté. Even so, the reader is not surprised to find that all lines of action come together at a point represented by Hortensia.

While Mario has been mooning over Hortensia, Ricardo, little older, but infinitely more experienced, has taken a more direct course of action. He becomes involved in an affair with Hortensia, who is willing to use either Ricardo or Mario as a way to get to Mexico City. But when she is forced by the boys' aunt to go live with her sister, an affair also develops between Hortensia and her sister's husband Efraín (it is not explicitly clear whether this is forced or welcomed); eventually Liboria will no longer allow her sister in the house.

The climactic event of the novel, which does not involve Mario, but which certainly affects him, is the death of Efraín. In this last section, vividly imagining the events leading to Efraín's death, Mario "sees" Efraín stumble up into the mountains to find a place to sleep and to enjoy the remains of his bottle. He stumbles, this time literally, upon Ricardo and Hortensia. (Rather unimaginatively, Hortensia has been meeting both Ricardo and Efraín in the same cave—the same cave, too, where once, had Mario only realized, his brother Ricardo tried to "give" Hortensia to him.) In a jealous rage, Efraín draws a knife, but is overpowered by Ricardo and Hortensia. Both are stained with blood in the struggle (hence Ricardo's stained jacket and Hortensia's compulsive hair-washing). They drag Efraín's body to the lake, throw it in—and wait.

There is a subtheme in *El sol* that for a long time seems extraneous (similar to the death of the cook's son in *La veleta oxidada*), the story of a mad, or saintly, hermit, who appears in the pinewooded mountains, living on berries and plants and occasional gifts of food. This hermit is found dead in a cave. There is a detailed description of his funeral, and of his wife's account of the vision that motivated him to dedicate himself to a hermit's life. (This light-filled vision echoes Mario's experience with the sun.) What seems strangely out of balance with the rest of the novella becomes obvious when the reader learns that Efraín, too, died in a cave: "[It was] a game, a fearsome web of interrelationships growing and unfolding into a drawing a fan that includes everything and there are the two caves the two corpses in eternal equilibrium ..." (121).

The review of events in Mario's mind, skillfully intermingled with the conversations of the other passengers on the bus—an interesting impressionistic passage—is really the end of the novella. There is no indication of what, if anything, will befall Ricardo and Hortensia for having killed Efraín, nor any hint of the future relationship between the two brothers, Ricardo and Mario. And truly these things are unimportant within the context of *El sol*. The reader's concern lies with Mario, with his new maturity, and his new responsibility, the "horrendous compromise" of knowledge.

We have here four works of prose fiction, and four quite different styles. *La veleta oxidada* is a mood piece, simple and poetic. In *El norte* Carballido employs an effective experimental structure to tell the story of an affair, and its ending. *Las visitaciones del diablo* is episodic, much more heavily larded with incident and action than the two earlier pieces. And *El sol*, actually, combines many of the effects of the earlier three works: like *La veleta oxidada* it is a mood piece, often poetic; there is some of the experimentation of *El norte* in *El sol*, and, again, the protagonist's disillusion in love; and, like *Las visitaciones del diablo*, *El sol* is to some degree reliant on a quasi-suspense format. One thing each has in common with the others, however, is a preoccupation with character. More than any other facet of his creation, it is apparent that Carballido is interested in what makes and breaks human relationships. For him, depth of characterization is much more important than wealth of acts or events, an attribute that one continues to see in his theater.

CHAPTER 5

Some Plays of Conventional Style: A Realistic Tetralogy

EMILIO Carballido has to date written sixteen full-length plays. Beyond that simple statement, it is difficult to categorize them for the purpose of discussion and analysis. It is difficult even to speak of them as a body of work. One cannot, for example, use the term "major" in referring to these plays, since that would imply that the shorter works are not their equal in quality. This is not true. "Yo también hablo de la rosa" is a "major" work, and superior to many of Carballido's longer pieces. The very early plays may be classified as either realistic or fantastic, but following the conscious experimentation of *La hebra de oro*—and although Carballido's style continues to be predominantly realistic—this method of classification becomes increasingly difficult. Many of the plays treating realistic subject matter are neither academic nor traditional in construction, and the term "realistic" is inappropriate. What we see, really, is that because of Carballido's variety and diversity, we can arrive at no satisfactory groupings of plays based on the division between realism and fantasy, on structure or technique, or on subject matter. The plays, then, will be considered in approximately chronological order, with the following exception: one basic difference exists among the works; seven plays do not fall within the convention and tradition of Mexican theater. For purposes of discussion, and not entirely satisfactorily, these plays will be called nonconventional, and the remaining, more traditional works, conventional.

There is one further rule to be adopted in examining the external components of a Carballido play: there is an observable correlation between structure and mood. As a general rule, the three-act works are the most realistic of the full-length plays.

In contrast, those pieces that are divided into *jornadas,* or those that in some other way deviate from the traditional three-act structure, either employ elements of the fantastic or for other reasons fall into the category called nonconventional. Carballido's use of the *jornada* is conscious: he has explained that "the *jornadas* correspond to the structure of the act as it was known during the [Spanish] Golden Age: the JORNADA, to be precise, as it was employed by Calderón and Lope, multiple changes of place, numerous scenes. Thus the *Pollos* is in one *jornada.* And the 'Rosa' is in one *jornada.* I use acts in those plays that are structured more academically, like *Rosalba, Felicidad.*"[1] Only one of the nonconventional plays is of three acts, and it is the first play Carballido ever wrote, *Los dos mundos de Alberta.*

I A Comedy

The first four of Carballido's full-length produced plays were of the structure he has called "academic": *Rosalba y los Llaveros* (1950), *La sinfonía doméstica* (1953), *Felicidad* and *La danza que sueña la tortuga* (both in 1955). All four are realistic in both style and detail. Frank Dauster has suggested that *Rosalba, La danza,* and *Felicidad* form a realistic trilogy.[2] It is equally appropriate to state that the *four* plays constitute a realistic tetralogy. Dauster's failure to include *La sinfonía doméstica* in the grouping may have been based at least in part upon that play's resounding lack of success.

Rosalba y los Llaveros[3] is a provincial comedy with a traditional situation-conflict-climax-resolution. Its protagonist, Rosalba, is a young girl whose "modern views" about sex, psychology, and the rights of the individual seem particularly advanced in contrast to the attitudes of the provincial branch of her family, the Llaveros. Rosalba and her mother Aurora arrive for a visit with the Llaveros to find that over the years the family has retreated into virtual isolation. Their fear of social disapproval has forced them into passive acceptance of a static existence. Their social inhibitions have three sources, one illustrated through the principal plot line, the others depicted through two minor problems that are less convincing dramatically, as well of questionable value structurally. The main issues center about

Azalea, the illegitimate child of Lázaro Llavero, the Llavero's
son, and Luz, a family servant. Luz, Azalea, and Lázaro are
all, each in different manner, the victims of moral blackmail.
One of the secondary plot lines concerns social status and racial
prejudice, and is developed through the relationship between
Rita, the Llavero's daughter, and her suitor Felipe. This problem
is not uncommon in Mexico, but it is not essential to the development of the main plot. The third source of the family's social
embarrassment is a mentally deficient aunt. This character,
Nativitas—who prefers to be called Incarnation of the Cross, an
appelation more closely befitting her preferred status in the eyes
of the Lord—provides a comic element, but her role as it relates
to the play's principal dramatic line is extraneous, and is justifiable
only as a means of emphasizing the false values underlying the
basic cause for the family's problems. Rosalba's function is that
of catalyst; she is the outside agent that stirs the family into
frenetic activity, resulting in a vitally altered social unit. The
Llavero family will never return to the same stultified existence
they were living prior to Rosalba's visit.

These three lines of action provide opportunity for a large
amount of comic complication which Carballido utilizes to the
fullest. The principal conflict lies in the contrast between the
Llavero's passive acceptance of life and the commitment to action
so basic to Rosalba's character. The complications and entanglements increase in steady tempo to the traditional moment of
climax at the end of the second act. Motivated by the sincere
desire to improve the situation of each family member, Rosalba
instead creates such confusion that she incurs everyone's wrath;
she seems destined to ostracism. In the third act, however, the
entanglements are methodically disentangled and a predictable
resolution effected.

Rosalba y los Llaveros is not Carballido's best play, nor would
we expect it to be. As his first successful play, however, we find
it interesting that this work signals a direction that has persisted
throughout Carballido's career: the comedy of manners consti-
tutes perhaps the largest single body of Carballido's writing,
both in narrative prose and in theater.

The flaw of *Rosalba y los Llaveros* is its very competence. It
really has no *weight*, although this criticism may elicit anguished

cries from the public who go to the theater only to be entertained. Well-crafted, the play is nevertheless frothy and superficial. It is also marred by what is probably Carballido's least convincing curtain line, which is spoken by Rosalba: "It's such a beautiful morning . . . the whole world could be young. In fact, the whole world is young. Let's go! (All exit, running; fireworks, music, and bells; they have reached the climax)" (247).

Rosalba's mother is fluttery and featherbrained. Felipe and his sister would be more effective if they were not so Indian in appearance and action. Lázaro is a provincial lout whose sudden liberation from his family and emergence as Rosalba's potential lover is not justified by past behavior. Rosalba herself is too cute, too blithely presumptuous, too *ingenue*, to be taken seriously, so that the action she initiates and perpetrates cannot be taken seriously.

Regarded within the framework of its culture, which is certainly the most reasonable critical approach, one can understand the play's success, and the reason for its continuing popularity. In Mexico, as in many other parts of the world, there is a certain validity in dramatizing backward and provincial social conditions. In this play, however, theme is not enough, and in spite of the fact that it treats such questions as illegitimacy, moral blackmail, and the rights of individuals, there is an old-fashioned quality about *Rosalba* that makes it seem much more dated, for example, than a play by Isben. *Rosalba y los Llaveros* is amusing and well constructed, but it cannot transcend the smallness of its plot. We see here the potential of Carballido's comic genius, but this is Carballido the talented young writer; Carballido the artist will emerge later.

II A Burlesque

La sinfonía doméstica (1953)[4] is the play that Carballido describes as having enjoyed a success "something akin to the sinking of the Titanic."[5] The play is not the disaster Carballido's comment would have us believe, for as a burlesque, a marital situation comedy, it has its good moments. *La sinfonía doméstica* was inspired by some lines from Richard Strauss: "My next symphonic poem will illustrate a day in my family. It will be in part lyric, in part rustic—a triple fugue presenting three themes: papa, mama, and child."[6]

The "three themes" in *La sinfonía doméstica* depart from Strauss's original intent; here they have become the themes of three women: Luz, Teresa, and Mercedes, the three "wives" of Efrén Mercado. The setting is appropriate for the burlesque tone of the play, a hotel that has fallen on bad days and into bad ways—renting rooms by the hour. As Efrén Mercado attempts—finally and inevitably, without success—to juggle his three wives, we are reminded of French bedroom farce, and the "ladies of the night" passing through the scene do nothing to detract from this similarity.

In addition to the three women, Luz (the mother-and-wife), Teresa (the sexpot), and Mercedes (the liberal and intellectual), and to Efrén (the rooster in this hen house), there are two additional major characters: Efrén, Jr., and Antonio, the hotel proprietor, friend of Efrén and secret admirer of his "wife," Luz.

The major portion of the first act involves the conscious accidents that bring the three women together. Luz arrives, penniless, drawn from the small town of Paso del Macho by Antonio's offer of financial assistance (Efrén, Sr., has defaulted on his financial obligations, and Antonio—selfishly?—has offered to help), and by the desire to prosecute Efrén for bigamy (Antonio has sent Luz a newspaper clipping of Efrén's "wedding" to Mercedes). Teresa arrives in the company of Efrén himself; Teresa believes they are celebrating their honeymoon. When Antonio berates Efrén upon his arrival with still another woman, Efrén answers that "this business with Teresita isn't going to last very long" (20). Nonetheless, Antonio insists that if Efrén does not return home with Luz, he will take Luz to see the second wife, and help her prosecute her complaint of bigamy. When he receives no assurance of either imminent or potentially permanent marital fidelity from Efrén, Antonio calls Mercedes to come to the hotel.

The second act is a series of near misses and, finally, actual encounters among the three "wives." Efrén, in a magisterial display of macho mumbo jumbo, convinces Luz that everything is all right and that he intends to return home with her; in the meantime, he tries to spirit Teresa out of the hotel—which she has settled into with all the delight of her new role as "wife" and perhaps older, but equally delightful, role as solace for her husband's sexual desires. At the same time, Efrén is contending with Mercedes, whose main concern now seems to be that Efrén must be brought to account for the injustices he has committed against *Luz*.

These first two acts work very well within the context of burlesque; it is only in the third act that both the level of comedy and of farcical suspense breaks down. There is too much "business" in this act, too much new information, and too little purposeful direction toward the obligatory farcical "solution." Efrén's effort to keep the three wives separated is drawn out too long; Antonio confesses to Luz his love for her; Efrén and Antonio have a fistfight; Mercedes threatens Efrén with a bigamy suit to avenge Luz, and states her general disregard for the state of matrimony; an enchanted Efrén suggests they fly away together; Mercedes proposes to Luz that she divorce Efrén; Teresa appears on the scene, and seemingly with no motivation other than that of escape, Efrén runs away with her, abandoning the two women to whom he had promised to remain constant; Mercedes announces that she is pregnant; Antonio tells Luz the hotel really belongs to her; and Luz, weeping that she will "never be able to do it," ends the play as she begins by renting rooms to "short-term" guests.

In a hand-written note on the manuscript dated some years later,[7] Carballido has sketched out the possibilities of alternate endings: one, that Efrén will flee alone, abandoning all three women; two, that Efrén and Teresa leave, as in the first version, but that Teresa comes back to the hotel, abandoned in turn, calls the police, and, after some consideration, the newspapers. In this version, the play will end with Luz's speech: "I must get Efrencito ready. I wouldn't want them to take his picture looking like that."

In addition to their interest as a bit of literary history, these notes indicate Carballido's obvious awareness of the problems of the third act. However, to this date, *La sinfonía doméstica* has been neither revised nor revived, and if we accept Carballido's own metaphor, it may lie forever rusting on the floor of the ocean.

III An Irony

It has been suggested that *Felicidad*,[8] which won the Ruíz de Alarcón prize as the best play of the year 1955, is a study of mediocrity. It is equally a commentary on egotism. It is not mediocrity or a lifetime of penury alone that have prevented the protagonist of this play from achieving the happiness every human seeks in some way or other, but rather his blinding egocentrism, his consuming self-pity and self-concern. Mario Ramírez Cuevas is a victim not of society, but of his own petty nature.

Felicidad consists of three acts and an epilogue. The epilogue may be of questionable dramatic value, a matter to be raised following a brief resume of the play.

The protagonist of *Felicidad* is Mario Ramírez Cuevas, a middle-aged teacher who looks older than he actually is. He dominates his wife, Cuca, who exhausts herself trying to prevent any situation that will afford her husband an opportunity to air his impatience and bad temper. He is disliked by his daughter Ofelia who resents his past and present stinginess, as well as the fact that he provided her with an education for the sole purpose of his own personal benefit. He is tolerated by his son-in-law Sergio, who considers him a bore and tries to escape evening after evening's account of the same problems and experiences.

This family, which has always lived in financial peril, is experiencing a particularly difficult period. Mario has received an advance in position, but the bureaucratic red tape accompanying the change has prevented his collecting his last seven salary payments. In addition, Mario has hoped to cash in a paid-up savings insurance policy, but has been deterred by the company's unwillingness to honor the policy with a lump payment, suggesting instead a monthly allotment. Ofelia and Sergio, who are expecting a child, would like to borrow from Mario enough money, when cash at last becomes available, to set up a small pharmacy in their home, where Ofelia can utilize her pharmacist's license, and from which they can derive a supplementary income that will prevent their repeating the financial history of the older generation.

At this time Mario meets Emma, a clerk in the office where

he tries every day to collect his back salary. From an entirely human impulse, Emma expedites his papers and Mario receives payment of his back salary. Egotistically, he is convinced that Emma has done him the favor because she is attracted to him, and sets out to pursue his advantage. Poor faded Emma—a "real dish" in Mario's conversations with his son-in-law Sergio—has zealously guarded her virginity to offer in exchange for marriage. Mario tricks her into a weekend in Acapulco, implying *he* will marry her.

During the period of planning, and until the ensuing consummation of the Mario-Emma affair, it is the wife Cuca who "profits" from her husband's rejuvenated sexual interests. We are embarrassed by her pitiful gratitude when she discovers some verses intended for Emma but which she believes inspired by her new relationship with her husband. At the same time, Ofelia's and Sergio's hopes for their pharmacy are doomed by Mario's determination to squander his accumulated salary on the weekend in Acapulco with Emma. At the end of the second act, Sergio tells his wife about her father's planned escapade; then Emma tells her mother; Mario's house of cards is about to come tumbling down about him.

The very brief third act is essentially the denouement of the crisis resulting from the revelation of Mario's infidelity. After the Acapulco interlude, Emma is summoned to the home by an anonymous letter sent by Ofelia and Cuca. A painful confrontation ensues between her and the family, and at this point in the action every character in *Felicidad* is suffering the unhappy consequences of Mario's affair. Sergio is embarrassed for having betrayed his father-in-law's confidences and thereby caused the confrontation. Cuca is a bitterly disillusioned woman; her husband's infidelity is made doubly painful by her own misinterpretation of his sexual preenings. Emma is humiliated, her promised marriage vanished into air, her carefully guarded virginity wasted. And Mario's very real pain is so obvious that even Ofelia, whose resentment has taken the most active form of all those offended, regrets her actions. It is at this moment of the family's lowest ebb that the representatives of the insurance company arrive to present, in full, the long-awaited savings policy. Mario, his hands filled with money, stands dazed and diminished at the moment that should signal his greatest *happiness.*

The epilogue to *Felicidad* raises some questions. It depicts a contrite Mario setting forth on a second honeymoon with Cuca, although still grieving over the loss of Emma; an Ofelia who is intent on not giving birth until her parents are safely away on their trip; and a philosophical Sergio who points out to Ofelia that "Your father would never have been happy anyway," and "Your mother always has been happy ... the little she's had in her life is what she's wanted, what she herself chose" (58). We have already seen Mario's unexpectedly sincere remorse and regret when confronted by Emma. The only new information in this segment is that Mario has decided to lend the money for the pharmacy to his daughter and son-in-law. This action softens considerably the harshness of the third-act ending. Perhaps the upbeat tone is necessary for a comedy, but as a result the character of Mario is rendered less believable.

Whereas in *Rosalba y los Llaveros* we find complexity of plot and oversimplification of characterization—a mode exaggerated in *La sinfonía doméstica—Felicidad* displays simplicity of plot and greater exploration of character. Carballido has delineated the personality of Mario with the care he devoted to the untangling of linear developments in the two preceeding plays. From the moment of Mario's first appearance (He wipes his feet. He shouts. "Is dinner ready?" [18]), Carballido builds up damning evidence of the man's supremely selfish character. He builds this evidence through the comments of other characters, and also with the irrefutable testimony of Mario's own utterances. The many references to Esteban, Mario and Cuca's dead son, are also intended to underscore Mario's stinginess and inflexibility, as the picture drawn of this father-son relationship is extremely unflattering to Mario.

One of Cuca's remarks about Mario illustrates the tyranny of her husband's character; it is the cold acceptance of her words, her resignation, that make this speech so effective: "Yes, it's true, he's selfish, and he's stingy, and that's just plain ugly" (46). None of the statements by other characters, however, says more about Mario than he reveals of himself in the following examples. He says to Cuca, as she is rushing to prepare his dinner: "Stick your hands in with the beans and boil them, and that way we'll have turtle soup" (20). Expressing regret for having wasted money on Ofelia's schooling, he says: "What did we spend our money for? Some help she is. Getting herself pregnant the first thing" (21–22). When he first meets Emma, he lies:

EMMA: You're married?
MARIO: I? Oh, no. (23)

A few lines later, he adds:

MARIO: Well, I do have a woman in the house.
EMMA: Is that right!
MARIO: I don't mean that! She's . . . just a woman, you know, fat, and as old as the hills, who looks after my things. (24)

When he is proudly recounting his adventures to Sergio, he says:

SERGIO: Well, but what will happen after the trip to Acapulco? What will you do with her then?
MARIO: Oh, later. . . . We'll see. I don't mean to go on seeing her after that. (41)

And to deceive Emma into going to Acapulco:

EMMA: Of course I want us to get married. That's the only thing I want.
MARIO: Oh yes. Well. That's what I want too. (45)

The viewer cannot help but feel pity for Mario in his hour of desolation, even if it is but the pity one feels for any injured beast. But the self-concern evident in his last words is ample testimony to the fact that he is still the egoist, lacking the redeeming qualities of humanity and nobility. "Twenty-five years, right? That is what I have after twenty-five years. Happiness! And what am I going to do now?" (57).

One wonders, too, what his wife and his cast-off lover will do now. Carballido may have intended for us to empathize with Mario—and the epilogue does serve to make him more human—

but *Felicidad* remains a searing portrait of a selfish man whose family has granted him greater affection and understanding than he deserves.

IV A Dream

Rosalba y los Llaveros has a provincial setting, though Rosalba and her mother come from Mexico City. *La sinfonía doméstica* is set in the city, though many of its characters are from the provinces. *Felicidad* takes place in "Mexico, D.F." *La danza que sueña la tortuga*[9] returns to the provinces for its locale, to the provinces and to the theme of the complex interrelationships of a provincial family that is so predominant in Carballido's writing.

Seemingly every Mexican family has a maiden aunt who serves as auxiliary nursemaid or chatelaine to the more fortunate members of her family. The Moredias are no exception. They have two aunts, Aminta and Rocío. The usual generational strata have been displaced in the Moredia family, with the result that at the age of fourteen Víctor became the head of the family. He acted as father to his younger sisters, so that he is wont to refer to them as the "sisters" of his oldest son, Carlos. Beto Joya, another nephew of Aminta and Rocío (but not Carlos's brother), shared approximately the same childhood with the two women. In other words, in ascending order of age, the principal characters are Carlos, an eighteen year-old university student, Beto, age twenty-nine, Rocío, thirty-six, Aminta, forty-six, and Víctor, approaching sixty.

The action in *La danza* is based upon a misunderstanding. Essential to the misunderstanding is the quickly established fact that Rocío is hard of hearing. The genuine love and affection between the nephews, Carlos and Beto, and their two aunts is also made clear early in the action. This unselfish auntly devotion is especially appealing to the young men because of the domineering character of Víctor, Carlos's father, and the smothering possessiveness of Albertina, Beto's mother.

The misunderstanding develops from a conversation between Beto and Rocío. Beto is repeating a conversation held earlier with his mother. To emphasize her disapproval of the girl Beto is planning to marry, his mother suggested that Beto would be much happier with a girl of Rocío's character and interests. Rocío hears only the part about herself. She believes that Beto is proposing, and all the pent-up longing and love she has always felt for him flows from her lips. Beto is trapped by his very real regard for his aunt and his desire not to hurt her feelings. He dares not tell her it is not she he wants to marry.

These events take place in the first act. The rest of the play evolves from this specific problem. There is an interesting structural difference between this and the previously discussed realistic plays. In them, and in the traditional pattern, the moment of greatest dramatic intensity occurs at the end of the second act. The third act then trails off in a descending curve. In *La danza*, a graph depicting the rise and fall of intensity would show a build-up to a climactic scene in each of the three acts.

In the second act this scene develops from the disclosures by Aminta and Rocío concerning their "engagement." When Víctor hears the news, his reaction is to bully and harass Rocío. Albertina, Beto's mother, tries to shame and humiliate Rocío. Neither of these two believes for a minute that the worldly, affluent Beto would marry his spinsterish aunt. Because of their cruelty, and their contemptuous assumption that there could be no understanding between Beto and Rocío, Beto makes a public proposal, apparently sealing his future to that of Rocío.

In the third act it is a blissful and blooming Rocío who effects the ultimate resolution of the problem. Beto has almost come to believe that their marriage would have a chance for success. Víctor, however, is chagrined that his family authority has been threatened, and that Beto and Rocío will marry even without his permission. He challenges Beto to a duel: "This is a matter for he-men, Alberto Joya. My sister is not going to be dragged off by the first lowborn son of a gun that wants to take advantage of her" (201). When Beto and Víctor exit, Rocío hysterically picks up the small pistol Víctor has given the two ladies for their protection, first aims at the departing Víctor, falters, then points the gun at herself, and finally empties the gun into the ceiling. This is a climactic and effective scene. Aghast at how close she has come to having committed murder and/or suicide, desolated by the prospect that either her brother or her fiancé

could be killed in a duel over her, Rocío makes an heroic re-
nouncement: she cancels the wedding in a masterful scene of
sincere emotion and high comedy.

One of the main reasons for the success of *La danza* is that the
characters are so convincing. The two maiden ladies, who could
so easily verge upon the sickeningly sweet, are given proper
perspective by Carlos, who loves them, but who also questions
the possibility of being able to *live* with them:

> CARLOS: I love them both very much, but have you really con-
> sidered what it would be like to live with them? With both of them,
> all day long?
> BETO: But I'm not here all day long.
> CARLOS: Yes, but every time you'd come home, there they'd be,
> singing their little duet as if you didn't exist, and buzzing around
> you like two honeybees. (197)

One is also amused by the humorous, but touching, childishness
of the two ladies at the end of the play. Stripped of the prospect
of "their" marriage, they are nevertheless emboldened to demand
that Víctor allow them to set up an apartment in Mexico City,
ostensibly to look after Carlos. Rocío, in spite of her grief, is
entranced by the idea of being able to go to the movies every
day. And besides, there is the glimmer of a hope that in the city
she may meet "someone else."

Further verisimilitude in Carballido's characterization is found
in his treatment of Beto. Beto, it is true, is motivated primarily
by sincere love for Rocío, but there is enough selfishness in his
gradual acceptance of the idea of marrying her to make him a
man, not a knight on a white charger: "I'm very. . . . I travel a lot.
I'm not a homebody. Very often I'm in a bad mood. What I'm
really trying to tell you two is not to expect too much from me.
I'm not even very affectionate, if you understand what I mean.
And I'd like you to leave me in peace" (192).

Víctor, too, is real. He blusters and shouts and intimidates
his children. He is a fanny-pincher, and proud of it. But he is
truly fond of his sisters. He loves his children, and his actions,
although often disastrous, usually result from a determination
to do what is right according to his viewpoint.

La danza que sueña la tortuga has an inventive story line developed by characters who are believable, and indeed, memorable. The provincial setting does not prevent enjoyment by an audience unfamiliar with the particular qualities of Xalapa, Veracruz. The viewer experiences honest and moving emotions, as the specific evokes the universal. Any moments that might have become mawkish are saved by Carballido's unerring sense of the comic. The best of this tetralogy of realistic comedies, *La danza que sueña la tortuga* is a vital play, Carballido's most successful venture in these early works of conventional style.

CHAPTER 6

Five Plays of Conventional Style: An Interplay of Sunshine and Darkness

I Las estatuas de marfil

IN 1960, opening a new decade of dramatic production, Carballido's attitude toward theater, perhaps toward the purpose of theater, seems to have become more serious, and following the four comedies of family or marital complications, he wrote, still in the realistic vein, *Las estatuas de marfil*.[1] This play brings together a group of people whose common interest is amateur theater. Of the characters, only Argentina, the mother of the protagonist Sabina, seems content to be herself. The others have either assumed roles that they present to the world as reality, or they are in the process of "trying on" the facades they would like to present. Each has a "frantic need to be someone else" (20). The Godoys are typical: Lucía is a snob who pretends a culture and sophistication that are obviously a veneer. Her husband, Gordo, plays the clown to cover the feeling of inadequacy that dates from his discovery of being cuckolded.

César, an author from Mexico City who has come to the provinces to direct amateur theatricals, is one of the three central characters. At first, he seems to be very much in command of himself and his situation. Through his own words, however, he reveals that his role of accomplished dramatist is a sham. The "successful dramatist" exists only in provincial Orizaba, where compared to amateurs he appears knowledgeable and experienced; among his fellow professionals in Mexico City his stature is considerably diminished. César forms a triangle with Sabina, the protagonist, and her husband Edmundo. The emphasis in this triangle is not upon a conventional compe-

104

tition for Sabina's love, although in the last scene between César and Sabina, they speak of "what might have been." In this respect *Estatuas* might also be considered a play about marital complications; but more importantly, the two men represent conflicting attitudes toward woman, specifically, Sabina. Sabina (an older Rosalba?) is a woman with aspirations that transcend her role as wife and mother. In the person of César, she is offered an opportunity for a theatrical career that will satisfy those desires. She must, however, choose between her present obligations and the opportunity for personal fulfillment. But Sabina's dilemma is larger than her own specific problem. She represents any person who must face the unhappy choice between obligation to others and personal need.

Edmundo, Sabina's husband, feels inferior to her; he is often gross, and in today's terms, a true chauvinist. Only occasional moments of honest sentiment, which he undoubtedly interprets as weakness, save him from being a caricature. His nineteenth-century attitude toward the role and responsibilities of a wife makes no allowance for Sabina's ambitions. Sabina is intrigued by the glimpses of freedom she sees represented in César. What Sabina intuitively knows, Edmundo must be told:

CÉSAR: I have always believed that in spite of marriage, husband and wife are still individuals with wills of their own—not slaves. (95)

CÉSAR: There are women who live intensely through the movies, who enjoy the pleasures of the bed, and who when they grow old find everything they need in the collective hypnosis of the rosary. And then there are women who do not, women who want something more, who discover music, theater, motherhood, science. . . . There are many ways to live intensely: they are all valid. What is impardonable is to mutilate ambition, to castrate will, to violate, and rape, and impoverish lives, and to deny the right to error and self-determination. (98)

In the second act, Sabina appears to have found the opportunity for a compromise. She continues to work with the group, inspired by the probability that they will compete in a festival in Mexico City and that she will be seen by people important in the theater. She continues with the convention of her marriage, though her relationship with Edmundo has badly deteriorated. At this point in the drama, however, Sabina becomes a victim of her biology; she finds that she is pregnant, and she knows that the timing of the performance in Mexico City will prevent her participation. For a brief period she is reconciled to the disappointment. She seems to believe Edmundo when he tells her that for a long while he has wanted another child. Then comes the trivial incident, the instant, that changes lives. Edmundo's conscience betrays him. An involuntary gesture calls Sabina's attention to a container of prophylactics in their dresser drawer. She does not need to examine them to know that they are defective and that Edmundo has tricked her. Founded in deceit, her condition is twice bitter.

Sabina does not want the child, especially a child conceived in Edmundo's selfish desire to dominate her and thwart her career. She finds support in something César had said earlier: "To bring a child into the world is not the act of animals. It requires the prior desire and love of the parents to whom it will be born" (26). Sabina's situation presents an interesting ethical question. Does she (and all the compromised individuals she represents) have the right to choose, to direct her own fate? Her problem is based upon deception. Is the moral decision the one that challenges moral convention?

Sabina capitulates. At the moment of decision, morally abandoned by César, she is not strong enough to stand by herself. We find that César, an idealist in the abstract, is in his personal dealings a pragmatist. On the professional level, he decides to scrap the play in which Sabina had the lead and present one in which there is no part for her—a play written by César, a much more attractive opportunity for him. On the personal level, he realizes that he lacks the conviction necessary to pursue the relationship that might have been the greatest of his life. He is a coward, but he knows himself very well, and this may be *his* salvation.

Betrayed by both Edmundo and César, Sabina will resort to a typically female revenge. She tells her mother:

It will be a boy. And he will be independent, and won't be afraid of anything. No one will stand in his way. I want him to be selfish, hard—like marble, not wax. Even if he makes me suffer . . . Sabino. Sabino Rojas Morel. Because Mundito is like his father. But no one is going to stop this one from being what he wants to be (with increasing possessiveness), because I will be with him always, looking after him; he's going to be mine. No one else's, mine, mine, mine. . . . (123)

Carballido implies that this terrible revenge will be a reality as long as women must satisfy their own needs through the accomplishments of their children. Sabina herself is the product of a frustrated mother. César is intelligent enough to understand what is happening, "Do you want the chain to continue?" (119); at the same time, he helps forge the next link. Who is the more guilty, César or Edmundo? Or Sabina, who will not rise above her personal disappointment to break the chain?

The title, *Las estatuas de marfil*, refers to one of the parlor games the childish Gordo tries insistently to make everyone play: "Well . . . you have to take a pose. . . . You stand like a statue, see? And the others try to make you move. You're like marble, and they turn you into chewing gum. Like this . . ." (40). It is clear that there is no one in the play who is "made of marble," although this is what Sabina proposes for her unborn child. The poses the characters have assumed—wife, artist, mother, macho—are nothing more than their goals, rigid, statuesque facades for the troubled, weak, and insecure beings who dwell behind them. Carballido, like Rodolfo Usigli in *El Gesticulador*, and Octavio Paz in *El laberinto de la soledad*, questions the approximation of "reality" and "role" in Mexican life.

It is possible to read *Las estatuas de marfil* as a drama à clef. The play is dedicated to Carballido's own *maestro*, Celestino Gorostiza, and in many ways the career of César duplicates Carballido's own. *Estatuas* begins with a rehearsal of *Los frutos caídos*, written by Carballido's close friend, Luisa Josefina Hernández. And the great role that was to have changed Sabina's life was that of Victoria in Marcelina Dávalos's *Así pasan*. . . .Carballido, through the character of César, also uses this opportunity for a number of caustic comments about the Mexican theater:

I'm just an apprentice author in a country where the theater supposedly has been "emerging" for the last twenty-five years. (37)

Not in Mexico, no: nothing somber, nothing disagreeable. If you
present life as anything other than a big meringue, you disturb the
journalist's digestion. The first commandment of the always-emerging
Mexican theater: Optimism! Smiles! Don't perform Ibsen! Death to
Strindberg! The second commandment: DECENCY! Down with the
Celestina and Aristophanes, because the bureaucrats in the Censor-
ship Office are offended by "bad" words. Also decent journalists.
And one mustn't treat sexual themes, because everyone in Mexico
is chaste! And the family! The holy Mexican family! Little mamacita,
the Mexican mother! How can you perform Medea? And patriotism!
The only government you can criticize is that of Porfirio Díaz.
Careful! Don't say anything about the present government, we don't
want them to shut down the theater. There's also the League of
Decency, and the Opus Dei, who permit obscenity as long as it
has no significance. It's good to excite the public, but careful!
Don't think there's anything transcendent about sex. Let them see
Letraz, but bann Ugo Betti. (59–60).

Perhaps Carballido is to some degree César. We certainly
know that Carballido is critical of certain aspects of Mexican
society, and of restrictions placed on theater by government.
But Carballido the social revolutionary also can be seen in
many other works: *Un pequeño día de ira, El día que se soltaron
los leones, El relojero de Córdova,* and *Silencio, pollos pelones,
ya les van a echar su maíz,* among others. Thus, it seems more
prudent to deduce the character of the author from all of his
creations rather than to identify him with a character in one
individual work.

II *Sunshine: A Satiric Farce*

Most of Emilio Carballido's plays are vivid testimony to the
fact that he is a sworn enemy of the institution, of any organized
force that oppresses or belittles the individual. In the three-act
romantic farce, *Te juro, Juana, que tengo ganas* (1965)[2] he
takes aim against the educational system, whose imperfections
are often a source of irritation to him. It is not the school
as a center of learning that offends Carballido, but rather the

school as an institution for the dispersement of false ideals, and as a factory of repressive values. Such a school is the setting for *Te juro, Juana*, which takes place during an academic recess in the year 1919.

Diógenes Feria, the director of a small, second-rate private academy, is a man of ideals. He holds as virtues the superiority of man over woman, the superiority of Diógenes Feria as an individual, moderation in all bodily appetites, discipline and strictness as necessary to the development of character, and the classic as the intellectual ideal. His perfection is tarnished considerably by the facts that he maintains his sense of superiority by denigrating others, that he is lecherous and penurious, that his character is founded on bluster and misguided self-esteem, and that his intellect is rooted in the dried-up debris of the past.

Diógenes has transferred a number of his precepts to one of his assistant teachers, Librado Esquivel, who agrees with Diógenes's belief that institutions are more important than persons. Librado halfheartedly pursues a "spiritual" relationship with Diógenes's daughter Juana (not unaware that this union will assure his inheriting the school directorship); at the same time, he pursues, in a more literal connotation, one of the students whose hunger for knowledge is more sexual than academic.

Juana Feria is the product of forty years of her father's adages: "You are not actually stupid, but a woman's intellect cannot be compared to a man's" (25), and "Therefore, I quote the German philosopher: women are short on ideas and long on hair" (25). Juana may be subjugated by her father but she has an unquenchable spark of romanticism which exhibits itself in several ways. She is the anonymous author of a frivolous little book entitled *Los caprichos de Chuchette* (her father has been firing critical salvoes at this "trash" in a critical column he writes); and also, with tender care, Juana has been nurturing her idealized romance with Librado that is about, she believes, to burst into bloom: Librado is on the verge of proposing. There is, however, one serious impediment to the romance, and that is that Juana is not free to marry.

The fly in the ointment—the gadfly—is Estanfor Vera, a nineteen-year-old student in Feria's academy. The year before, Diógenes accidentally had surprised Estanfor and Juana in a moment of intimacy, and in good nineteenth-century fashion had locked him in that same room while he summoned a judge, and forced them to marry on the spot. From the moment of that traumatic experience, Estanfor has been an annoyance to everyone. His encounters with Juana are characterized by resentment and rancor. When Juana asks him to allow her to get a divorce so she can accept Librado's proposal of marriage, Estanfor refuses to cooperate. He demands in return a forged degree from the academy and a recommendation signed by Diógenes. Diógenes stubbornly refuses to be blackmailed by such an insolent pup of a student and despoiler of daughters, and by the end of the second act the conflicting desires of each character seem to have resulted in an impasse.

The farcical solution of *Te juro, Juana* illustrates the saying that "The ideal couples are never those that people imagine" (82). When Librado learns that Juana is the author of a "pornographic" novel, and when Diógenes is arrested for assault as he tries to remove all the copies of the book from the libraries, Librado beats a fast retreat. He escapes directly into the claws of Inés, a voracious sex kitten. However, after Juana is lionized as a result of being exposed as an "exquisite and entertaining" author, and when Diógenes is exonerated from criminal charges, Librado tries to reinstate himself in their affections. He recognizes his mistakes too late, however, and the momentum of inescapable pairings off rolls onward to the end.

Diógenes is eventually worn down by Evangelina, a librarian who has for years been stalking him. Librado finds he cannot escape from Inés as easily as he succumbed to her. And Juana and Estanfor, extreme opposites in every way, realize that they complement each other so perfectly that they must be the ideal couple. An aged maid states the moral of *Te juro, Juana*: "Punishment is being allowed to continue our lunacies unto the end, to obtain what we take to be happiness; if that happens, we never know what true happiness is" (83).

As befits a farce, the humor in *Te juro, Juana* is broad, based on sight gags, running jokes, puns, and the satire of outmoded customs: witness the mad reunion of the lovers:

JUANA: Librado.
LIBRADO: Juana.
JUANA: Librado!
LIBRADO: Juana!
JUANA: Librado. . . .
LIBRADO: Juana. . . .
JUANA: Won't you sit down?
LIBRADO: Thank you very much. (20)

An amusing running joke is based on the conjugation of the Spanish verb *abolir*, to abolish. The one queried always begins confidently with "yo abuelo" (*abuelo* can mean either "grandfather" or "I abolish"). The butt of the jest gets as far as "tú abuela" (which is a specific and very crude allusion to certain acts one would wish never to be performed upon one's grandmother), and invariably retreats in red-faced disarray.

Estanfor is the most comic of the characters. His behavior is comic, his situation is comic, and he is the vehicle for the longest running joke in the play. He constantly metathesizes the syllables of his words so that "municipios," for example, can become "supinimio" or "suminipios" or "pusinimios." This difficulty affords numerous opportunities for puns and tongue twisters.

Like many farces, *Te juro, Juana* has an underlying serious vein. Carballido despises hypocrites like Diógenes and Librado, and by ridiculing them so effectively he demolishes their pretentiousness. Also, by placing the action at the turn of the century, Carballido exaggerates the theme of woman's *non-liberation*, a problem with which Carballido is extremely sympathetic. In some ways, *Juana* resembles *La danza que sueña la tortuga*. *Juana*'s Diógenes is the *Danza*'s Víctor exaggerated to a farcical degree, and Juana and Estanfor parallel the reverse December-May relationship of Rocío and her nephew Beto, although the love affair in *Juana* does reach fruition.

Finally, the sensuality in *Te juro, Juana* is the most pervasive of any of Carballido's preceding realistic works. Every character is either lecherous, teasing, repressed, or yearning for love. *Sex* is the main character, and the repression of healthy and natural instincts is the villain. The song from which the title

is taken suggests the essential mood of *Te juro, Juana,* a dashing
and daring sentiment for the early years of this century:

> Tomorrow, Juana, in early morning,
> I'll wait for you, Juana,
> And you know where.
> I long for a glimpse of your beautiful body,
> I swear to you, Juana,
> Oh, Juana, I swear. . . .
>
> A toe or an ankle,
> Your knee . . . or your thigh,
> I swear to you, Juana,
> Oh, Juana, I'll die. . . .
>
> I'll wait for you, Juana,
> In early morning,
> I'll wait for you, Juana,
> And you know where . . .
> I'll wait for you, Juana,
> Oh, Juana, I swear. . . .

III   *Darkness:* Acapulco, los lunes

Unlike the highly entertaining *Te juro, Juana* (written with
the obvious intent to entertain) and the ebullient, lyrical "Yo
también hablo de la rosa"—both dating from 1965—Carballido's
next two plays, *Acapulco, los lunes* and *Conversacion entre las
ruinas* (both dated 1969 following a hiatus of several years),
are bitter and pessimistic. Neither work has the least trace
of gaiety, hope, or good humor, and in neither can we find a
sympathetic character.

Acapulco, los lunes[3] begins with an alarming and confusing
concatenation of shots and screams, an escaped tiger, and
milling crowds of film extras, the most dramatic opening
Carballido had employed in his realistic full-length dramas,
and designed to confuse, startle, and even irritate his audience.[4]
This hectic scene serves to introduce to the audience, and to
each other, the three principal characters: Myra, a North American, a former airlines stewardess making a marginal living

by occasional modeling and intermittent water ski lessons; Alvin, also an American, an indecisive and insecure refugee from the draft [during the period of United States involvement in Vietnam]; and the Mexican Lucio, who is working as an extra on the film set. An immediate affinity is established among these three who live precariously on the fringe of Acapulco's affluence. *Acapulco, los lunes* hinges upon the shifting patterns of attraction and aversion among these three characters.

The fourth character, Liuba, is a strange and free spirit whose love of snakes and animals is a distant echo of the intermediary in "Yo también habla de la rosa," and of Ana in *El diá que se soltaron los leones*: "Those who believe in evolution maintain that its progress is always forward. . . . That isn't true. No, that isn't true. Evolution also marches backward, and we never know which is which" (p. 22).

Liuba's close association with her nonhuman companions, as well as her sometimes animalistic approach toward congress with her human companions, weaves in and out of the main line of action, but her function, rather than being directly involved, is more that of a commentary that questions our accepted lines of demarcation between the animal and human worlds.

Finally, there are the tourists who serve collectively as a kind of Greek chorus, and as individuals as well. Essential to both the tone and action of *Acapulco*, the tourists are the game upon which the four semipredators prey. The tourists sustain Acapulco, but as they sustain, they also maim. In response to a query following the completion of the work, Carballido wrote: "I believe it could be, with very few differences, *Capri, On Mondays*, or *Bangkok, On Mondays*. . . . The case is that Lucio . . . is pushed to his conduct by a general situation, pushed by that attitude that poor countries adopt in order to receive foreign currency in the form of tourists: they convert their countries into brothels."[5]

Essentially, *Acapulco* is concerned with the methods of survival employed by Lucio, Myra, and Alvin, victims or predators, depending upon one's point of view. Of the three, Lucio is the most generous, sharing with his American friends the meager, always transitory earnings derived from his calling as a gigolo; he is also the most honest. He accepts the terms of his "profession," and is justifiably annoyed when Myra and Alvin piously protest the source of his generosity but willingly accept its practical rewards. At one point Lucio comments (the familiar litany of thousands of Mexicans invaded by hordes of wealthy North American tourists):

All of you grow up with silver spoons in your mouths. You have everything. Everything is super clean, super plentiful . . . super movies, supermarkets, super everything, everything in hygienic tin cans, purified water. . . . That's why when you leave there you're not good for anything. Except spending money . . . when you have any money to spend. You're big crybabies about everyting. Nothing's good for you, it gives you malaria, or diarrhea, or fever, or gonorrhea, or sunstroke . . . or remorse. Why don't you all go home? (29–30)

In spite of the reiterated protestations of their "principles," Myra and Alvin drift into active participation with Lucio's schemes for cheating tourists, their compatriots as well as equally gullible visitors from other Latin American countries. They begin with relatively harmless swindles such as selling "toucans" whose colorful cardboard bills begin to disintegrate almost as soon as the sellers have vanished, and whose bills of health turn out to be applications for primary school. In a second sequence, Myra and Alvin sell faked pre-Colombian idols, a familiar enough racket. They enter more hazardous territory when, in one of the world's oldest confidence games, Lucio poses as Myra's jealous husband and threatens a terrified tourist with a year in jail for adulterous involvement with his wife. Myra, who knew she was setting the tourist up for *something*, had not been informed of Lucio's actual intentions. She tells Lucio she does not in the future want to be involved in any similar schemes, but she accepts her share of the blackmail money Lucio collected from the tourist, and soon is again embroiled in Lucio's plans.

What finally forces Myra and Alvin into a new course of action is a still more serious offense. Lucio administers a Mickey Finn to one of his white-haired companions and then steals her traveler's checks. Myra and Alvin fear being directly impli-

cated in this crime because Myra had picked up the pills and
Alvin had told the woman his real name.

The next morning Alvin and Myra go to the police station;
to protect themselves they inform against Lucio, their friend
and provider. When the wealthy American lady denies that
she has been robbed, Alvin and Myra are left with their own
humiliation and their dread of having to face Lucio, who is
aware of their betrayal. Although he is cleared of their accusa-
tion, a routine check administered while he is being held in
jail leads to the discovery that Lucio is driving a stolen car.
In a rather abrupt and not completely explained ending, Lucio
goes to prison, as Myra, Alvin, and Liuba head toward rosier
futures. Acapulco? Well, Acapulco is . . . Acapulco:

> TOURISTS: (sing)
> Gin Rickey, Grasshopper,
> Old Fashioned, Silk Stocking,
> Planter's Punch, Whiskey Sour,
> Dry Manhattan, Golden Hour.
>
> Golden Fizz, Royal Fizz, Silver Fizz,
> Aquavita, Sangría
> Screwdriver, Margarita,
> Orange Blossom, Daiquiri,
> Side Car, Bacardí.
>
> French Cocktail, Submarine,
> Tom Collins, Rum Collins, Rum Conga,
> Stinger, Zombie, Tonga.
>
> Acapulco Sour
> Acapulco Sling
> Acapulco Blossom
> Acapulco Gin
> Acapulco Collins
> Acapulco Fizz
>
> Acapulco! Acapulco! Acapulco!
>
> Acapulco!

And so the tourists will continue to flock to Acapulco to victimize Mexicans who in turn will victimize their victimizers.

In *Acapulco, los lunes* Carballido has posed a serious, if familiar, moral problem. There is little doubt that he sees in Lucio a victim of the artificial society imposed by foreign wealth, the product of the resultant clash between two disparate cultures. A scene near the end of the play makes very clear Carballido's vision of his character: Lucio performs a personally dangerous but completely selfless and compassionate act for a fellow prisoner, echoing his earlier unquestioning generosity with Myra and Alvin.

The two North Americans are odious—weak, parasitical, unprincipled, and disloyal. The thesis seems clearly defined: Lucio is a metaphor for Mexico, and Myra and Alvin represent the malignant influence of the affluent North American culture upon a poorer and more naive southern neighbor. In spite of the obvious superficial truth of this assumption, the proposition contains a flaw, and we call attention to it here not for political argument, but because it speaks directly to the effect of the play. In posing and answering his moral problem, Carballido has offered only half an answer. Myra and Alvin are weak and unattractive; one might even call them evil. But although Lucio is more attractive than they, and although he is honest in his appraisal and acceptance of his existence as a gigolo, a cheat, and a thief, this does not make him a hero. There *is* no heroic character in *Acapulco, los lunes*, and Carballido offers no real solution to the dilemma he poses. It is the very insolubility of the vicious circle of victimized-victimizer that makes *Acapulco* such a bitter and pessimistic play. In this light the enforced gaiety of the cocktail chorus of the finale is sobering rather than intoxicating. The merry vacationer who has witnessed *Acapulco, los lunes* may regret that memory in the next bar in Capri, or Bangkok... or Acapulco.

IV *Conversation in Darkness*

Conversacion entre las ruinas[6] continues the darkness of *Acapulco, los lunes*, although it is a very different kind of play. In contrast to the occasionally frenzied activity of *Acapulco,*

Conversacion is basically static, a quiet, albeit highly emotional, conversation between two characters, Anarda and Antonio, former friends and lovers (is the similarity of their names meant to suggest a Siamese twinlike, star-struck inseparability?). Antonio's servant Enedina plays an important role in the single *action* of the play, although she speaks very little, and is present on stage only four times.

In many ways, *Conversacion* is the simplest play Carballido has written, and structurally it resembles the flashback of prose fiction. Antonio and Anarda speak of the past which is the heart of the play, the past that casts its dark shadows over the lives of Anarda and Antonio.

Anarda has followed Antonio to the jungles of Oaxaca where he is working as a laborer in a sawmill. His wants are provided for by Enedina. Anarda wants Antonio to return with her to "civilization," to pick up the threads of their past lives. They talk about this past. Enedina, hearing Antonio tell Anarda that he will never forgive her, kills Anarda who dies in Antonio's arms.

There are no acts, no scene divisions, in *Conversacion entre las ruinas*. The two principal characters converse; Enedina, quietly and submissively, moves about the fringes of their conversation.

ANARDA: We lost the house. It hadn't been ours for a long time . . . it was his . . . César's. He got well. César got well, did they tell you? (11)

ANARDA: [to Enedina]: Antonio cleansed me. (18)

ANTONIO: [to Enedina]: I went because her father was a very famous man. He was a writer. . . . An enormous family, and César, Anarda's husband (20). We returned, often . . . until one day I stabbed Anarda's husband, twice. (22)

ANARDA: Are you sorry? (28). I came to take you back. There is no charge against you. (30)

ANTONIO: It was to do the act in your place, to prevent you from committing a crime. (39)

ANARDA: Nothing mattered anymore, because he had bought me and used me like an object. (41)

ANTONIO: I waited. Until I saw him come down the stairs. I leapt upon him. And *you* turned on *me*, shouting, cursing me, pounding me with your fists. And you threw yourself upon him, to protect him. (44)

ANARDA: I came to ask your pardon. . . . I came to stay here with you (45). Don't make me go back. (47)

ANTONIO: After that night, my only wish was that it had been you. Because I have never forgiven you. (48)

ANARDA: I'm going to stay here. Until you forgive me. Or kill me. (48)

Enedina enters. . . . Without hesitation she stabs Anarda, twice. (48)

ANARDA: Am I going to die? Antonio! Am I going to die? (50)

Conversacion entre las ruinas is that most difficult of theatrical forms, an absolutely static situation—except for the knifing—in which the dramatic tension must be evoked from the actors' accounts of past emotions and past events. And Carballido does not entirely avoid the difficulties inherent in the form. Almost inevitably, speeches become monologues as each character reminisces, recounting his or her memory of their shared experience. One wonders whether *Conversacion entre las ruinas* would not have been more successful as a short story, whether it would not have lent itself more readily to the flexibility of that genre. And if it were to be presented as drama, one wonders whether the past events could not have been more successfully acted out, rather than narrated. As it stands, the difficulties of the form are an encumbrance that do not allow the dramatic tension to emerge effectively.

Conversacion is a very personal play. Carballido's dedication reads: "In this work is hidden the memory of beloved persons, of their ambience, of their magic. I do not paint their portraits; nothing in the plot alludes to them. But I hope to have captured here the intensity of certain days, of our conversations, of our affection."

In spite of the warm tone of the dedicatory words, the "landscape" of this play lay in ruins long before Antonio and Anarda began the conversation that Anarda, at least, hopes will lead to a renewed life together. But no new life arises from those sterile ruins. With the fatal thrust of the knife, Anarda is silenced forever, and Antonio, with the silent Enedina as witness, is destined to recite an eternal monologue amid the darkness of the ruins.

V *Return to Sunshine*

Un vals sin fin sobre el planeta[7] is a return to sunfilled years, to the early boyhood when an adolescent protagonist still enjoys the luminous beauty that is life's gift to the innocent. *Un vals* is Carballido's second play about the Moredia family of *La danza que sueña la tortuga.* It seems more than coincidence that these lighthearted plays carry titles expressing the joy and freedom of the dance.

The events of *Un vals* precede by four years those of *La danza.* Carlos, a university student in *La danza,* is fourteen years old in *Un vals,* and his father Víctor and his aunts Rocío and Aminta are correspondingly younger. Beto Joya, who through a chain of events beyond his control found himself engaged to his aunt in *La danza,* does not appear in *Un vals.* Víctor's young wife Guille, the mother of his second family and absent in *La danza,* is an important character in *Un vals.*

In addition to the two plays, the Moredia family appears in one of Carballido's short stories, "Los huéspedes." *Un vals* is, in effect, the dramatized version of the story, and contains whole sections of identical dialogue. This is not surprising considering that they were written at approximately the same time: "Los huéspedes" appeared in *La caja vacía* in 1960; the manuscript of the play is dated 1957/1970.

A young couple who say they are brother and sister come to the Moredia home offering for sale a rather valuable set of antique jewelry. These young people, Consuelo and Gabriel, tell the Moredias that they are attempting to reach the bedside of their dying mother from whom they have been separated for a long time.

In reacting to this story, the Moredia family is divided along lines of family loyalties. The romantics of the family, Carlos and his two aunts, are completely enchanted with the pair. They are attracted by their beauty, and touched by the story of the upper-class father, a government official, who had never married the poor and powerless mother. Guille, although she is very interested in the jewelry, is suspicious of the young pair, and is disposed to dislike them if only because Carlos, Aminta, and Rocío are so taken with them. She is backed up in her suspicions by a neighbor who also distrusts the guests, and who thinks she has seen Consuelo's picture somewhere in the newspapers.

Víctor, the dominant force in the Moredia family, takes the part of the romantics for various reasons; partly because he is not indifferent to Consuelo's attractions, partly because it pleases him to play the role of the kind and generous philanthropist. He offers Consuelo and Gabriel the hospitality of the Moredia home for the night, and in addition he himself pays for their tickets to Chiapas. After Consuelo and Gabriel leave, Guille's suspicions are confirmed when her neighbor brings a clipping from a newspaper that identifies Consuelo as the wife, not the daughter, of Diputado Corzo, and, adds the neighbor, "since the wives of government officials always are driven by chauffeurs, that Gabriel was surely the chauffeur!" (52). The important message of *Un vals*, however, is that not even these revelations will disenchant Carlos, for he has been touched by the magic of the guests, and whenever he remembers them, he will hear the music of their waltz.

Un vals is entirely faithful to the short story, with one exception. Because of the limitations of the dramatic form, an important dream sequence is necessarily treated differently. In both the play and the short story, Carlos's perception of Consuelo and Gabriel is linked with an awakening sexual awareness. In both, this awareness is experienced in a dream. In "Los huéspedes," Carlos "was awakened by an electric discharge... his thighs were wet and sticky... he understood: the hygiene classes, the exciting words: puberty!" (36). Since the playwright is limited when describing what goes on in the mind of his character, the dream sequence in *Un vals* is external, and is greatly expanded.

The characters enter a set lighted only by moonlight. Their paths intersect, but they do not see one another; they speak, but they speak only to themselves. Rocío and Aminta "dream" of the past when they were young and their mother was still alive; they protest their condition; they feel tied down by their responsibility to Víctor, to his wife, and to his children. Guille "dreams" her jealousy; she feels that she is an outsider in her own home; she resents the fact that Carlos and Rocío and

Aminta exclude her from their inner circle, and supplant her even in the affections of her own children; she is distressed at Víctor's interest in Consuelo, and sure that his generosity is based on more than innocent gallantry. Víctor "dreams" of his responsibilities: "The house with its interweaving dreams. The house is sleeping, the house on my shoulders" (48). Carlos "dreams" of his resentment toward his father, who was unfaithful to his mother: "You had two homes, and mother knew it" (49). Within his dream, he tells Gabriel and Consuelo of a different dream: "I dreamed about you and I spurted all over everything" (47). Consuelo and Gabriel appear on a round platform beneath a brilliant spotlight, joined as if they were a single two-headed being covered with scintillating ornaments. They resemble the dancing image of Shiva. Carlos worships them. The god-figure divides into Consuelo and Gabriel, and they leave on the train. Carlos rises, replaces them on the platform, and very slowly, "like a weather vane," he begins to whirl to the rhythm of the waltz.

In her dream, Aminta says, "And dreams are real, too. After dreaming something, we're never the same again" (53). Thus Carballido implies men's lives are shaped by their dreams, and Carlos's dream was in three-quarter time. Somewhere in the person of Carlos, the university student of *Un vals*, and somewhere within the Carlos the reader does not yet know, the sunny cadences of the waltz will echo endlessly, and his life will be forever influenced by that rhythm.

Within the mode of the conventionally constructed play, Carballido has demonstrated his diversity in the nine works beginning with *Rosalba y los Llaveros* and ending with *Un vals sin fin sobre el planeta*. His settings are varied, physically and temporally, and his mood ranges from the comic to the romantic, from the light to the dark. This continued inventiveness, which is indicative of the scope of Carballido's interests and talents, is illustrated even more vividly in the following seven plays of nonconventional style.

CHAPTER 7

Seven Plays of Nonconventional Style: A Theatrical Voyage to Other Worlds

I Voyage to the Inner World of the Mind

OF his first play, Los dos mundos de Alberta (1947),[1] Carballido has said: "I do not *ever* intend to publish them [it and "El vestíbulo"], but I am fond of them; there are no other copies. As you are interested in them I will let you read them, but NO ONE IN THE WORLD has read them . . . except for my contemporaries who knew about them at the time, and of course have forgotten them by now."[2]

This hitherto first and unknown play is of great interest, particularly because it is written in a style that Carballido later perfected in works like "El espejo" and "Medalla al mérito." The title of the piece accurately describes the concept: Carballido began his career by attempting to portray on stage psychological as well as external realities.

Alberta is a young girl who to escape a dreary and sordid reality has retreated so far into a world of fantasy that she can no longer perceive which is the real world. She lives in a tiny, squalid apartment that she shares with a bitter, disillusioned, and immoral mother. Three additional characters inhabit this world: Nicolás, the boy friend who is the mother's exclusive preoccupation; Jorge, a young man who spends a great deal of time with Alberta, and whose motives the mother suspects; and Rubén, a neighbor and friend upon whom the mother depends for occasional small loans.

The story line is simple. Alberta dreams that she is a princess; in this dreamworld Jorge becomes the Supreme Captain of the Royal Armies. But in the real world Alberta's existence is bounded by the cleaning and cooking chores she must perform

122

for her mother and Nicolás. She is so "gone," as her mother describes her, that she is incapable of functioning in any more demanding capacity.

The boy friend Nicolás has tired of the mother and tolerates her only because she supports him. He demands a large sum of money, threatening to leave for the north where he can find work. The mother, desperate to hold Nicolás, tries to borrow the money from Rubén. Rubén demands some security. The mother has nothing of value, except Alberta. So, in effect, Alberta is sold to Rubén. The mother, who is never given a name, tries to find Nicolás but he has already left town. Drunken and desolate, she returns home to find Rubén and Alberta together. Alberta begs the mother to forget Nicolás, and to save her from Rubén. Together, she says, they can go away and start a new life. The mother seems swayed by true maternal emotion, but Rubén convinces her that as soon as Nicolás learns she has the money he will return to her. The mother's decision, sadly, is predictable. Believing she can still find Nicolás, she rejects Alberta. Alberta, her last tie with the real world broken, seems to faint, but as Rubén carries her to the bed a black-veiled figure emerges to stand by the head of the bed; we know that Alberta is dead.

This series of events could obviously be portrayed realistically, but Carballido is not satisfied to depict merely the sordid external reality; his greater desire is to explore the interior world of Alberta's mind. In order to do so, he literally divides Alberta's being into two worlds. This division is represented in the stage setting: as she begins to daydream, the rear wall of Alberta's room rises to reveal a luxuriously appointed castle chamber. In the dream reality Alberta is duplicated in Alberta-the-Princess; a second actress enacts, and occasionally speaks, Alberta's daydreams. The character of Jorge also requires a second actor who performs the actions of the Supreme Captain of the Royal Army. Rubén does not appear as a character in Alberta's dreamworld, but is referred to symbolically as King of Bears. In both worlds Jorge/Supreme Captain promises to protect Alberta, but in Alberta's mind his caresses become confused with the threatening sexuality of Rubén/The King of Bears.

In *Los dos mundos de Alberta*, unlike the perfectly executed "Medalla al mérito" and "El espejo," the movement from the lower to the upper planes on the stage (the movement from the external world to the interior world of Alberta's mind) reflects some blurring of concept. The worlds are sometimes separate, with Alberta and Jorge on one plane and Alberta-the-Princess and Jorge/Supreme Captain on another, but at times they are confused, with Alberta and Supreme Captain comprising one pair and Alberta-the-Princess and Jorge the other. Therefore, the emotional pairing of the couples is not always paralleled in their conversational and physical arrangement, and the double planes that are so effective elsewhere in Carballido's work are here merely confusing.

Nevertheless, characteristic concerns are visible in this first effort. One is the attempt to break through the traditional limitations imposed on the playwright by the fact that the stage, unlike the strictly literary genres, presents an exclusively *external* reality to the audience. Normally, a character's thoughts—not what he recounts of those thoughts in speech—can be expressed only through nuances of movement and expression, a very limited and unsure mode of communication. Carballido attempts to rupture this convention through the use of dual planes and simultaneous action by two actors who represent the interior and exterior realities of one character.

A second preoccupation is the theme of emerging, and often dark, sexual awareness. In *Los dos mundos de Alberta*, this is manifested in Alberta's aversion to Nicolás, her mother's boy friend; in her memory, that she was deprived of her father's love because of sexual conflict between him and her mother; in her memories of a bear rug in her childhood home that is transmuted into the symbolic fear of Rubén, the King of the Bears; and in her confusing Jorge's sincere advances with the threat of sexuality as it is represented by Rubén.

Los dos mundos de Alberta offers an important new perspective on Carballido's theater as a whole. From the beginning, Carballido was attracted to the *non*realistic and the *non*conventional play: the unpublished "El vestíbulo" and *Los dos mundos de Alberta* dwell in the worlds of dream and death; "La triple porfía" depicts the struggle in a man's mind between

Reason and the Devil, the embodiment of temptation; "El triángulo sutil" can best be described as the dramatization of an idea; "La zona intermedia" takes place in a world of pure fantasy; and "Medalla al mérito" is a perfect example of the double-plane, double-world concept of *Los dos mundos de Alberta*. In all, then, Carballido wrote six plays before turning to the realist mode of *Rosalba*, a significant indication of his theatrical instincts.

II *Voyage to the World of Dream*

La hebra de oro (1955)[3] is not Carballido's best play, but it may be his most important. "La hebra," he says, "is quite important to me; it was the first time I attempted to join a realistic treatment with an imaginative one.... Before, I wrote works of one genre or the other, but never mixed together."[4] This statement must be examined rather carefully in view of the fact that *Los dos mundos de Alberta* is a similar blending of realism and fantasy. To resort to cliché, an author is not always the best judge of his own work. We could amend Carballido's statement to read "the first time I *successfully* attempted to join a realistic treatment with an imaginative one," although even this alteration excludes the successfully executed "Medalla al mérito." To accept Carballido's own assessment, we must make the following compromise: *La hebra de oro* was the first *successful* utilization of this style in a *three-act play*.

In *La hebra de oro* interest in the oneiric is more evident than conventional plot, and effect is more important than characterization. An apparently nailed-shut door that is completely sealed by cobwebs serves as entrance and exit for some characters; when forced open by others, it reveals a brick wall. Mental telepathy, rupture of the barrier between present and past, and a vaudeville magician's prestidigitorial display are only part of Carballido's theatrical pyrotechnics. One character utilizes a radio beam to enter the scene; if the radio is not turned on, he cannot enter. At one time the stage effects give the illusion that the entire set is whirling through space; constellations and the Milky Way can be glimpsed through the widows of the dizzily whirling house.

The elements of plot that emerge through the visual and oral assault of *La hebra de oro* are simple to recount. The play's six characters are divided into groups of twos. Two are indigenous to the rural site: Sibila, a young woman who seems condemned to produce weak and deformed children, and a ninety-year-old man, Salustio, the caretaker of this ranch in Ixtla. Two are visitors who have ties with the ranch but do not live there: Leonor Luna and Adela Sidel. Two are visitors from the nonreal world: *Man* and Mayala. The two elderly women have returned to a deteriorating property deeded in the name of their grandson. One of the grandmothers, Adela, would like to dispose of the land, but it cannot be sold because the grandson has been missing for several years. Leonor's motivation is her hope that she will see her grandchild once again before she dies. The appearance of a mysterious stranger (who is actually the grandson), accompanied by a female companion (who is Dream), signals the intrusion of the non-real world into quotidian events.

The identity of the stranger is revealed in direct ratio to the diminution of his strength; his death follows the revelation of his identity. After the incidents involving the intrusion of the nonreal in the play-within-a-play, the dream play, the action returns to the "frame" structure, the real world of the ranch. There Sibila runs away, abandoning her baby. As the curtain falls, Leonor is rocking the baby, whom she names Silvestre, obviously an allusion to the continuity of life.

The events of *La hebra de oro* are primarily a recapitulation of different facets of the past; there is little *forward* movement toward a denouement. On stage, in actual time, the outside, plotted play is not as long as the inner play, nor as important. One qualification must be stated, however: what the plot *implies* is important.

This implication concerns the possibility that a *place* may determine lives. An air of decay permeates the ranch. The gothic house is in disrepair; the fields are exhausted and no longer fertile. The Indians who work the land are surly and discontent. Only Salustio, who is practically a member of the family, remains loyal. When Leonor Luna asks the stranger (Silvestre) why he ran away, he says: "Because I couldn't stand the feeling of mourning" (94). (Remembering that the setting of this play is Ixtla, and considering the current vogue of Carlos Casteneda's mystic *Journey to Ixtla,* one cannot avoid speculating that perhaps the influence of place is more real than fantasy.)

In the reenactment of Silvestre's death and the scenes in which Leonor and Adela are allowed to view portions of their past, the *truth* of their lives and not their previous interpretations and rationalizations, produce a cathartic effect. The agony of the dream-reality-experience exorcizes their incubi. And Carballido's symbol for this new reality is seen in the last stage direction: "Something has burst from the sack of corn. It has been rising slowly since the beginning of the scene. Now it can be seen clearly: it is stalks of corn, many of them, which stretch upward while Leonor sings, and the curtain falls" (105).

The many planes of reality, and the many angles from which one sees the same characters and situations, are the most interesting features of this innovational play. For instance, one first sees a purely provincial setting: a decaying tropical estate, two very elderly ladies, an ancient family employee. But seen more closely, the estate is far from ordinary and differences are great between the two women. Adela is greedy, Leonor is generous. In the scenes reenacting the past it is revealed that Adela has never known a satisfying human relationship (and is therefore greedy), whereas Leonor has known love (so can afford to be generous). At the furthest point of their contrasting natures, it becomes evident that Adela is incapable of achieving any sort of communication. It is Leonor who is the vehicle, the *medium,* for their transportation into the dream reality. Her very name, Luna (moon), suggests the night and the unearthly. When we first meet Leonor she is sleepwalking, and in a flashback we learn that on her wedding night she was also sleepwalking, immersed in dream. She has always been an agent for the supernatural. Adela's last name is Sidel. Because of the moon-star relationship (*luna-sideral*), was Carballido unconsciously influenced in selecting her name? Because Adela is mutilated emotionally, did he "mutilate," that is, condense *sideral* into Sidel?

Like Luna, Sibila is another example of character prefiguration. Sibila *is* a sibyl. She is gypsy, enchantress, seer. It is believed that she casts spells on her own children, and for that reason they die. Of the four real characters in the "frame" play she is the nearest to the dreamworld. She flees at the play's end. Is that because she was one of the evil spirits exorcized by the cleansing effect of the truth revealed by *Man*? Certainly, she is sensitive to the other world: she is the first to recognize that the stranger is Silvestre.

Finally, to exhaust the game of name symbolism, there is Mayala, *Man*'s companion, Dream. Apart from the echoes of Maya, representing the Mexican's ties to a pre-Colombian past, ties that emanate from the very earth, another connotation resounds in the name. In Hindu, *maya* means "the origin of the world"; its secondary meaning is "the illusory appearance of the world."[5] Whatever the symbolism of her name, Mayala, along with *Man*, represents the spirit of the theater's patron, Dionysius. Part magician, part philosopher, part mortal, part revealer of truth, *Man* is a flashing, shifting beam of light. Mayala, the true representative of preoral, preintellectualized theater, is dance, grace, Woman, companion, and knowledge. *La hebra de oro* is a work that needs to be *played*, to be *experienced*. Perhaps as much spectacle as drama, it is unlike anything that had previously appeared in Mexico.

In these terms, the importance of *La hebra de oro* cannot be overstated. The continuing tradition in Mexican drama has been realistic; social and political problems have served as primary motivations and themes. During the era of receptivity to foreign influences and of the innovations following the founding of the Teatro Ulises in 1928, there was a shift in subject matter toward a closer inspection of personal, rather than societal, relationships, along with increased interest in problems of middle-class morality, but the *approach* remained basically realistic. A few exceptions exist: Francisco Monterde's "Proteo," Alfonso Reyes's only play, *Ifigenia Cruel*, Miguel Lira's *Vuelta a la tierra*, and Rodolfo Usigli's *El niño y la niebla*. None of these plays, however, was in any way a conscious effort to explore and exploit the world beyond sleep, which is the significant contribution of *La hebra de oro*.

Reminiscent of those balls of tiny mirrors that slowly revolve flashing splinters of rainbow light in smoky discotheques, *La hebra de oro* is dizzying to contemplate, but its light is perhaps too diffuse. Its positive values, nonetheless, overshadow any flaw. More than the one-act "La zona intermedia," which lies entirely within the framework of fantasy, more than the fantastic trilogy, *El lugar y la hora*, which has not to date been performed on the stage, *La hebra de oro*, in its first appearance in the Teatro Universitario in 1956, was a real landmark in contemporary Mexican theater. The two one-act plays "Medalla al mérito" and "El espejo" feature the same quality of reinforcement of the real through the use of the nonreal, and either is probably a better play than *La hebra*, but again, neither of these plays has been performed. For this reason, *La hebra de oro* may still be Carballido's most important and influential play, and one that will be studied as a real turning point in the course of Mexican theater.

III *Voyage into Wonderland*

El día que se soltaron los leones (1959), a farce in three *jornadas*,[6] is an inspired combination of superficial realism, surrealism, and imaginative technique. This play and *La hebra de oro* represent the peak of experimentation in the middle years of Carballido's career. *Silencio, pollos pelones*, written some years later, uses a similar technique, but as it is a more overtly political satire it does not have the effect of nonreality. Only in "Yo también hablo de la rosa," one of Carballido's more recent plays, does he return to a similar fusion of subject matter and technique.

El día contains elements of the silent movie, of Japanese stylized Noh drama, and of fairy tales with personified animal characters. Occasionally one notes a disjointed narrative style characteristic of Ionesco; one is, additionally, reminded of Brechtian goals and aesthetics; and the protagonist's dreary existence similarly recalls plays of social protest of the 1950s. These statements are not meant to suggest that *El día* is derivative, for it is an extremely original work; rather, it is an attempt to convey to some extent its variety.

The opening to *El día* is similar to that of any of Carballido's realistic dramas, *Felicidad*, for example, or *La danza que sueña la tortuga*. Ana could be another Aminta or Rocío or Adela; in her sixties, she has squandered her life caring for a whining, hypochondriac aunt. She has never received love; she has never known human concern. She derives her only warmth and affection from the companionship of a cat that lives in the kitchen, hidden from her fanatically disapproving aunt. Although supposedly bedridden, the aunt discovers the cat and chases it from the house. This is the incident that propels Ana into the world beyond the confines of her dismal existence.

As he did in *La hebra de oro*, Carballido implies in *El día* that place dominates events. Ana enters Chapultepec Park to search for her cat, and as she steps into the park she crosses a boundary into a world of enchanted creatures and absurd actions that seems more real than her everyday reality. Once here, Ana encounters a new freedom and never returns to her former condition.

In the park Ana meets a number of character types. *The Man*, for example, is an affable opportunist, a good-humored failure. Frustrated in his aspiration to become a writer—and one deduces that he has never taxed himself too greatly in the effort—he has become a bum, living in the park and extorting small sums from couples he "surprises" in the bushes. These characteristics contrast with those of the Señora, a typical Mexican wife and mother. Her altruism lies at the opposite pole from the Man's self-interest; she has dedicated her life to her family, but now she feels useless and wonders whether she has accomplished anything valuable. These two characters afford differing points of view on the question of personal responsibility and the sources of life's satisfactions.

In the "real" world Ana, like her neighbor and her aunt, is a realistically portrayed individual; the characters she meets within the park, however, are stereotypes. But in this play one-dimensional figures are appropriate and effective. They move always within a framework of fantasy; they are part of the enchanted world of the park. Furthermore, each emphasizes one particular quality, and each is therefore freed from the complexity expected of realistic characters.

In addition to the Man and the Señora, Ana meets a professor who represents regimentation and order, and one of his pupils who, regimented and ordered, is always addressed as if he were an entry in a rollbook: López Vélez, Gerardo. Inside the magic confines of the park, this student escapes authority to symbolize rebellion and freedom. Regimentation (professor) and rebellion (López Vélez, Gerardo) clash, as they are wont to do. López Vélez, Gerardo, flees. In order to create confusion to cover his flight, he frees the lions from their cages. Everyone in the park is caught up in the ensuing pandemonium. Many do not welcome this involvement, feeling they have done nothing to warrant such inconvenience, and even danger. But as the Man philosophically observes, "You never know when someone's going to let the lions loose" (282).

When it becomes apparent that the lions will be shot unless they are recaptured, Anna and the Man, who have established a friendly and protective relationship with the lions, have no hesitation in siding with the lions against the police who run madly through the park trying to round them up. On the other hand, the professor would like to aid in capturing the lions, thereby proving his valor "under fire." He offers his military "credentials" to the police, but is exposed when they are identified as bus transfers. Even though his "official" assistance is rejected, he continues to act in the light of his own view of his importance; he commandeers a portable sound system and wanders about the park warning the populace of the state of emergency. In the hubbub, he is mistaken for one of the lions, and shot.

The lions finally are cornered. Rather than see them shot, Ana leads them back into their cages. The Man, ever the opportunist, announces to the press: "*I* captured the lions. It was I. I captured them" (292). But now Ana makes the most important decision of her sixty years: she elects to join the lions in their cages: "The day will come when all of you will be in cages while we lions wander free, roaring through the streets" (292). Ana will spend her remaining days sitting knitting in her cage, a scruffy old lioness growling and throwing things at the children who come to the park to learn about life:

THE MAN: You hate the children.
ANA: No. They're marvelous. I love them very much; I would

rather play with them. But I shout to them like this so they'll learn. Do you think they'll ever know why I shout at them?
THE MAN: Not now. Later.
ANA: That's good. Brats! Ugly little worms! Stupid kids! (295)

It is not difficult to see the political implications in Ana's rejection of "normal" society in favor of the lions, and in her interest in "educating" the children she loves. This interpretation is substantiated in Carballido's own statement that the play was for him a catharsis of conflicting emotions regarding social- ism and capitalism. "There is nothing to do," he says, "except shout and tell the children not to be stupid, because . . . what can you do but shout at them, and tell them stories."[7]

In addition to being a political statement *El día que se soltaron los leones* is a modern morality play. Right triumphs and villainy is punished. *El día* offers its audience the same com- munal excitement that explodes into "Ole!" following a perfectly executed veronica in the bullring. Every injustice one has ever suffered at the hands of an unworthy antagonist is alleviated when Ana turns on the aunt who has bound her to years of servitude: "It's a very clean cat. Oh, Aunt, why can't I keep it? When you die, I won't be sorry. There isn't anyone in the whole world who will feel sorry. I won't. I'll fill your house with cats! And I'll take them in to urinate on your bed!" (257). López Vélez, Gerardo, the irrepressible rebel, wins the recog- nition he deserved for rebelling against the professor when he rescues a woman from drowning in the park lake. And satis- faction is the only possible emotion that could result from the shooting of the professor:

POLICEMAN: Who shot him?
ANOTHER: Who knows?
ANOTHER: Put him on the ground.
PROFESSOR: Not on the ground! I don't want to get my uniform dirty! (276)

There is not a line, a character, or an emotion in this play that does not contribute to the whole, and the whole is moral.
In *El día* the climax and resolution of the play evolve directly from the opening situation. It is inevitable that Ana would

elect to live among the "caged" lions and devote the remainder of her life to educating children who only *think* they are free to be wholly free. It is appropriate, too, that it is the search for her beloved pet that leads her from the confinement of the spiritual cage of her aunt's apartment to the freedom of the literal cage of the big cats.

Carballido's technique here is brilliant. He integrates action through music, choreographed movement, and mechanical devices such as projected color slides. From the time the lions are released until Ana leads them back to their cages there is *seeming* confusion on the stage, but every movement is carefully controlled: bands of slapstick police race back and forth; frightened citizens flee from imagined pursuers; the professor swings his loudspeaker among the crowds; shimmering banners of blue cloth are rippled across the stage to simulate water; boats are suspended from the shoulders of their rowers with openings for feet and legs that allow the porter to "row" freely about the stage; animals are portrayed by humans in deliberately unrealistic costumes. The intermission between the first and second *jornadas* is actually not an intermission but the screening of "A Day With the Lions," using film, animated drawings, or slides.

In his production notes to this work, Carballido says that the lights should be exaggerated and unreal, a blending of strong colors, but he specifies that this onslaught of light and color must never obscure or overpower the characters. He might have been speaking of his concept of the play itself, for from this dazzling totality of light, color, and movement, the play emerges as clean and seamless as an egg, a beautifully conceived whole.

IV *Voyage into Myth*

"I don't hope to be immortal, or any of that crap. I want to be a hero, and that's that" (84). Perseus, the protagonist of *Medusa* (1959),[8] Carballido's second myth-inspired drama, displays the same attitudes that characterize Theseus, the hero of the one-act play written two years later. "As long as I have anything to do with it, I don't intend to fulfill any oracle" (87). Like Theseus, Perseus' most intense desire is to be responsible for his own acts, to struggle, independent of the gods, to strive, independent of the gods, and to free himself completely from the restrictions of the fate which the gods have ordained for him. The implication resulting from a consideration of these two twentieth-century versions of Greek myth is readily apparent. Both heroes, or, more accurately, both antiheroes, removed from the orientation of god-controlled actions, assuming the onus of respectability for their own acts, emerge as cruel and relentless monsters. They are brutal and cold, seemingly incapable of either pity or love. Untempered by any trace of human concern, their ambition becomes a craving for pure power. By denying their commitment to their gods ("I shall exile all gods from my kingdom! They are detestable!" [133]), they themselves essay the role of gods. In exchange, they sacrifice a quality of inestimable worth: their humanity. Contemporary heroes cut off from both human *and* divine communication, they suffer the ultimate isolation.

Like "Teseo," *Medusa* is a formidable exercise in ingenuity. As he does in the briefer play, Carballido works within the absolute structure of the myth, but he is so imaginative in changing motives and attitudes that the myth assumes an entirely different meaning.

The early years of Carballido's Perseus are the same as those of the Greek Perseus. Son of Danae and Zeus, he and his mother are cast into the sea by his grandfather Acrisius, king of Argos, a ruler fearful of the prophecy decreeing his death at the hands of his grandson. Perseus and Danae are washed ashore on the island of Seriphos where they are offered the hospitality of its king, Polydectes. They live there until Perseus comes of age. It is at the moment of Perseus' majority that the two versions begin to diverge. The mythic Perseus kills his grandfather accidentally in the Olympic games. In Carballido's version, Perseus kills Acrisius with a discus, but the death is homicide, not accident. Although he had not premeditated the death, and although he had vowed not to fulfill the oracle, Perseus is betrayed by his own temper and willfully kills Acrisius in a fit of rage.

In the Greek myth it is Polydectes who sends Perseus to slay the Medusa. Perseus kills the monster, returns to Seriphos, and there also kills Polydectes. In Carballido's version it is not Polydectes who charges Perseus with the death of the Medusa, but Athena, who wants the head for her shield. (In Greek legend, the Medusa head does adorn Athena's shield.) In carrying out his charge, however, Carballido's Perseus falls in love with a Medusa whose fatal power resides in her snake-like hair. During the time her hair is bound in the Nefretiti headdress she often wears, Medusa assumes the appearance of normality. As in the case of his grandfather, Perseus does not wish to kill Medusa. He truly loves her, but he is once again betrayed by his own frailty. Because he cannot possess her exclusively, he kills her. After her death, Carballido's Perseus continues the events of the Greek myth: he slays the dragon who holds captive the princess Andromeda; he marries Andromeda, and then returns to Seriphos. There, still true to the myth, Perseus murders Polydectes by maliciously exposing the severed head of the Medusa. But now the fate of Carballido's hero is altered. His mother inadvertently enters at the instant he uncovers the Medusa head, and she, too, is turned to stone. Only with Polydectes did Perseus *will* his crime; the other three deaths occurred as a result of his attempt to direct his own destiny: "I *am* my heroic feats," he declaims (144). Perseus has aspired to be divine, but each time he has been betrayed by mortal frailties: anger, possessiveness, and malicious jealousy. Perseus has sacrificed the emotions that humanize mortal beings, but limited by this very mortality, he has failed to achieve the grandeur that places gods beyond any question of fallibility or responsibility. One is forced to ask: does Perseus represent Carballido's concept of twentieth-century man?

The three principal characters in *Medusa* are Perseus, Danae, and Medusa. Perseus *is* the protagonist, so we may wonder why Carballido has emphasized Medusa by giving the play her name. The most reasonable explanation is that of all the characters, it is the freakish monster Medusa who is the most human. She is Woman in all her qualities, both bad and good. And she understands love much more fully than Perseus ever will: "Look; man is alone; he needs a mirror that will say to him, 'You're somebody; you're beautiful. You *matter.*' That mirror is the beloved" (110).

Carballido makes his Medusa even more human by telling us that she was not born with the hair that turns mortals to stone. As a child she had beautiful golden hair, but the gods were envious of her and they punished her by making grotesque the feature she most prized, her long golden hair:

The gods do not operate in fits and starts. I contemplated my hair; I devoted all my energy and all my attention to it. Thus little by little, piece by piece, each hair became independent of the others. One day I saw two tiny eyes on the end of one hair. My nanny wept and screamed, and when she cut off the hair blood spurted from it, and the hair fled, slithering away to hide in the garden. It was she who fashioned this headdress for me. I fled from my home, and on the voyage, on the ship, my hair continued to grow thicker and thicker. When I arrived on these shores, it had reached the maximum of horror. For a moment I uncovered it and birds fell to the ground like misshapen hail, like stones. They were stones. A sailor who was swimming turned to a statue and sank in a froth of boiling water. This, then, was I: Medusa; no longer young, no longer one of the Hesperides. I met the Gorgons, my equals. That's what they called me: the "other" Gorgon. But they were born like that, I wasn't! I wasn't! (121)

In spite of all her sympathetic qualities, Medusa also represents carnal woman. Her actions are determined by the knowledge that "when it's almost dawn, there will be slaves willing to turn to stone in exchange for possessing me for an instant" (134). And because he cannot possess her for himself alone, Perseus beheads Medusa: "(He murmurs) Is that what you were? Was that you? And yet, I love you" (134).

Perseus' passion for Medusa is strong, and sincere, but it is no stronger than his love for his mother. The love scene between Perseus and Medusa evokes a kind of universality; man and woman, they seem to represent the love that exists between Man and Woman: "Somewhere, a man is kissing a woman. I can feel them. In every beat of your heart, I can feel them" (130). But Perseus experiences a much more specific and personal love for Danae. Whether or not Carballido intended it, his protagonist has an Oedipal complex.

Dubious of the authenticity of his mother's version of his

conception—"The warm shower of liquid gold that enveloped me, penetrated me" (85)—Perseus has known only maternal love. When he meets Medusa, he tells her that his main goal in wanting to become a hero is to remove his mother from the palace in which they are living (thereby ridding himself of his competitor, Polydectes). One of the things that angers him sufficiently to kill his grandfather is that the latter makes unflattering allusions to Danae; like a pouting child, Perseus shouts, "Leave my mother out of this!" (116). The entire fifth act is devoted to depicting the last stage of Perseus' disillusionment with his mother, the most severe blow inflicted in the long course of Perseus' self-destruction. He tells his mother: "I came here first; I wanted to take you with me; I wanted you to enter as a queen the kingdom that belonged to your father" (140). But Perseus arrives too late. Danae is pregnant, and she and Polydectes are belatedly celebrating their wedding. Perseus' reaction to this announcement is revealed in his gestures: "Raising his voice; with grotesque movements; gaining control of his emotions . . ." (146). After he accidentally kills Danae, Perseus addresses the stone image of his mother: "We are all turning into stone, little by little" (149).

So, in effect, all of the characters in *Medusa* are destroyed by Perseus. Danae, Medusa, Polydectes, and Acrisius are dead. Andromeda means nothing to Perseus; she is a mere appendage, a convenient target for his cruelty; she, too, will perish. But perhaps none has fared more cruelly at Perseus' hands than Perseus himself. He is virtually dead, his spirit "turned to stone."

The five-act structure in *Medusa*, in addition to suggesting the neoclassic Greek drama of Corneille and Racine, is beautifully symmetrical and necessary in itself. The first and fifth acts take place on Seriphos, while the middle three concern the major events that take place in the Gorgons' palace in Africa. In addition, the classic tone provides the framework for much of the humor in *Medusa*, a humor that grows out of the unexpected. There is nothing amusing about what happens to the characters in *Medusa*, nor in the play's resolution. The humor derives from the shock of nonclassic behavior within a classic setting, from anachronistic situations: Gorgons whose claws cause runs in their stockings; Danae, lounging in her bath, ordering her servants to bring her hairdryer; a slave in the marketplace selling "filthy postcards." One would expect a modicum of nobility in the companion to a god and mother of a hero. Instead, a vain and petulant Danae reminds one of an aging movie queen. Acrisius is the king of Argos; again, one expects dignity and nobility, but observes instead only the back-slapping, locker-room aggressiveness of a man who fears he has lost his virility. Of all Mexican playwrights, only Carballido has the deft sense of the comic that allows him to deal so humorously with intrinsically tragic events.

In writing of Perseus' fetishism (for to Perseus the head of the Medusa is as much fetish as it is weapon),[9] of his exaggerated dependence upon his mother, his sadistic marriage to Andromeda, and his grotesque love affair with Medusa, Carballido has created a striking study in abnormal behavior. But more importantly, he has created a frightening portrait of contemporary man—fearful, lonely, desolate in his isolation. Using the model of a timeless Greek myth, Carballido has created a twentieth-century classic.

V Voyage to the Twin Worlds of Prevarication and Invention

Although El relojero de Córdoba[10] was written in the same year as Medusa, it is a very different kind of play. Among the more superficial distinctions is the fact that El relojero is structured in two jornadas, Medusa in five acts. Whereas Medusa is darkly pessimistic, the tone of El relojero is predominantly optimistic. What the two works do share in common is their atmosphere of otherworldliness. Medusa, of course, was based on a Greek myth, and in El relojero, Carballido turns to the Orient, to the seventeenth century, to the Shantung province in China, and to a storyteller named Pu-Sung Ling, a writer whose brief tales are bathed in the aura of the Arabian nights, and whose characters at times reflect the wisdom of a Solomon. Carballido playfully acknowledges the source of his inspiration by introducing this historical tale-spinner into the fiction of his seventeenth-century Mexican drama when one of his characters, the magistrate Don Leandro Penella de Hita, mentions that he has a friend in China whom the events of the play would interest. The exotic mythic tone is paralleled in local myth: the allusion to a mulatto girl who traces the outlines of a ship on the wall of her prison cell and then sails away, for example, as well as several allusions to the mythic influences exerted by the land on which the city of Cordoba was founded. The atmosphere of *El relojero* is a blending of the colonial, the pastoral, and the Oriental.

The protagonist is Martín Gama, an insignificant man whose ambition is to construct the most magnificent animated clock ever built, all for the eternal glory of Cordoba—and Martín Gama. The true *hero* of the play, however, is an attractive, lecherous, wise, and witty magistrate, Don Leandro Penella de Hita, who does not appear until the second *jornada*. It is Don Leandro who extricates Martín from the problems into which his irresponsible actions lead him.

Martín, acting as agent for his brother-in-law, is sent from his home in Cordoba to buy some property in Orizaba; when he arrives in Orizaba, Martín, who has been entrusted with two hundred and fifty ounces of gold for the purchase, stops in a local inn, El Mesón del Aguacero, and there meets by accident an old school chum, Nuño. Nuño exemplifies everything that Martín dreams of being; he is happy-go-lucky, he has traveled to the courts of Spain and Italy, he is tremendously attractive to a women—at least, according to his own accounts— and he is successful financially. Martín, bolstered by the weight of the gold in his saddlebags, cannot resist trying to equal Nuño's tales. He displays his brother-in-law's gold, fabricating an adventure in which he portrays himself as having stolen the treasure from some poor wretch along the highway whom he then pushed over a steep precipice and killed.

The next morning Nuño and the serving boy in the inn, interested in the reward paid informers, denounce Martín before the tribunal, and Martín is led away to court. There he vehemently protests his innocence and explains the real purpose of the gold. The local magistrate, faced with conflicting stories, orders a search to ascertain whether the accused or the accuser is speaking truth. Unfortunately and unexpectedly, a headless corpse is found on the very site Martín had described. Trapped in his own prevarication, Martín is accused of murder.

In the second *jornada* both the coincidence of the discovery of the unexpected corpse and the solution to Martín's personal maladjustment are resolved. Martín effects his personal salvation by coming to terms with his limitations. He recognizes the discrepancy between what he has dreamed of being and the person he truly is. He says to his wife Casilda:

I haven't been *bad*, but it's because I wasn't able to. I never knew how. I watched everyone and I wanted to be like that, capable of the kinds of things people talk about when they say, "*He's* really sharp," or "*He* knew how to live." I married you . . . because I loved you. Because one day you fell as you were going into church and everyone laughed. Because your brother shouted coarse things at you in the street, and because one day when you saw me you dropped your shopping basket and nobody helped you pick up your vegetables. . . . And I was never capable of saying it. I wanted it to look as if I married you for your money. . . . (61)

Though now it is within Martín's power to achieve some internal peace, factors over which he has no control still exist: the mysterious materialization of a headless and unidentified body. The problem is resolved by Don Leandro after he arrives in Cordoba and finds the case unsolved. He offers a reward for the missing head, purportedly for purposes of identification. The head is found by Lisardo, a handsome shepherd Martín had seen briefly in the inn, and identified by a beautiful young woman named Elvira, who had already claimed the *body* as that of her missing husband. Don Leandro, with no little selfish interest, suggests to Elvira that she is too attractive to sacrifice her beauty in mourning, and since she is penniless, he offers to sponsor a new husband for her. He posts notice of his intentions, and Nuño and the shepherd who found the missing head appear to contend for the honor. With Solomon-like wisdom, Don Leandro proposes that the beautiful widow Elvira choose the one she prefers. She selects the shepherd, who is obviously both economically and socially inferior to Nuño. With that one act, Don Leandro finds the solution to the crime. He proves Elvira and Lisardo guilty of the murder of Elvira's husband. He punishes Nuño for falsely denouncing Martín. Thanks to Don Leandro's devious cleverness, and Martín's new self-awareness, Martín's salvation, both spiritual and physical, is complete.

The folktale quality of *El relojero* in some ways recalls Bertolt Brecht's *The Caucasian Chalk Circle,* also a reinterpretation of an old tale. Both employ music and song, demonstrating their belief that theater involves the integration of several art forms. In Carballido's play, as in Brecht's, the judge is the most appealing character; Carballido's Don Leandro exhibits the same characteristics as Brecht's Adzak: cleverness, wit, and a not too rigorous code of personal standards. In addition, the awareness of their role-playing is basic to each of these "implementors" of justice:

> MARTÍN: Is it true? Is it true?
> CASILDA: Your freedom, Martín!
> MARTÍN: Justice!
> DON LEANDRO: (smiling) Yes, Justice. (70)

These similarities are merely superficial, and Carballido demonstrates his originality in a most unusual structure and concept. *El relojero de Córdoba* contains *two* plays-within-a-play, one resulting from Martín's prevarication and the other from Don Leandro's invention. Don Leandro sets his play in motion as soon as he suspects that Martín is innocent and that Elvira may be involved in the murder of her husband. He may not know the ending of his play, but he knows that it will work out to its logical solution. Martín is the author of a much more complex drama. He *invents* a play, the fictitious story of an assault and a robbery, and then is amazed and disconcerted to find that he is the protagonist in an actual series of events that parallel his invention. So there are two prevaricators in *El relojero,* and two inventors, and the difference between them may simply be a question of the difference between naiveté and experience. It is doubtful that Martín *realizes* that he is a character in an internal play—a play in which he is director as well as actor—in the same way that Don Leandro consciously directs his play-within-a-play in the second *jornada.*

Both Martín's and Don Leandro's plays resolve themselves through one action: Don Leandro's offer to sponsor a husband for Elvira. The subsequent identification of the body convicts the wife and lover, frees the innocent prevaricator, and satisfies the wise magistrate. The clockmaker returns to his clocks, a changed and wiser man.

VI Voyage into Black Humor

Silencio, pollos pelones, ya les van a echar su maíz! (1963)[11] is Carballido's most overtly satiric and comic play. It is not structured in acts, but is continuous in action, relying on lights and commentary to effect changes of scene and time. A male and female actor, Coro D and Coro E, act as chorus; they comment on the action and set the stage by describing the situation at the opening of various scenes. They are from the beginning participants in the multiple characterizations of the piece. They establish no personal attitudes and change character as easily as they change scenes.

Silencio, pollos pelones is Carballido's trenchant humor at its best. The cast pokes fun at everything holy: literature, elections, authors, politicians, death, the naively pretentious acts of the poor, charity itself, the audience, and themselves. The many parts are played by three actresses, A, B, and C, three actors, A, B, and C, and Coro D and Coro E, all of whom establish their personalities in the introduction to the play:

Sly, vulgar, Actor A walks forward and addresses the audience.
ACTRESS A: (Refined, cultured) I learned my lines, and they're *divine*. Shakespeare, no less. (511)
ACTRESS C: (With enthusiasm) Sartre, Anouilh, Dürrenmatt, Frish, Williams, Miller. I *adore* Tennessee Williams! I played *La putain respetueuse* . . . in a performance at my school. (512)
ACTOR B: (very informed [following a long discussion of the areas in which Mexico is underdeveloped]) The trouble is that Mexican *authors* are underdeveloped. (512)
ACTRESS B: No, it's that the authors believe they're the only thing that counts in a performance. *I* say, where would they be without us (the actors) and without you (the audience)? Although, *you're* not terribly important. (512)
ACTOR C: "Because the play and its creator should comprise a complete universe." (511)

To which Coro D adds this choral explanation: "Apollinaire. From the prologue to his work. . . . (Hesitates, overcome with modesty) 'The Tits of Tiresias!' (To the horrified shock of the other actors) That's what it's called!" (512). The story concept on which the play is based is dark but extremely humorous. It concerns the death of a man by drowning and the events that develop after his body cannot be found; and without a body, there can be no funeral. The family is too poor to afford a wake. A misguided social worker, unable to obtain financial assistance and meaning to express sympathy, donates a coffin. This "gift" assumes the proportions of a monster, until the ingenuity that arises from necessity suggest a solution that is advantageous to everyone concerned. This concept first appeared in the title story of Carballido's collection of short fiction, *La caja vacía.* In the short story it is the condition of the family and the disillusion of Doña Leonela that command Carballido's attention. The family's poverty is dramatically underscored by the inefficacy of governmental action, and Doña Leonela's failure as a government social worker is contrasted to the success of her privately funded charitable foundation. These same elements appear in the dramatic version, but here the political aspect is expanded and emphasized. Elections, *gringos,* political strong men, officious clerks, the "deserving poor" themselves—all are vulnerable before Carballido's blisteringly humorous attack. Statistics, "as exact as the official statistics from which they were taken" (510) are used in a most entertaining way: "Some 47.66% of the population wears shoes; if everyone had but one leg, the government could provide shoes for almost 96% of the population" (514).

With an effective and fluid style Carballido blends scene into scene with the same dexterity and agility with which his actors move from character to character. Gesture, posture, and characteristic garments suggest character in the same way that moveable "rooms," posters, and flats suggest setting. The scope of the play demands versatility from its actors and imagination on the part of the choreographer, set designer, and director, and in his appendix, Carballido acknowledges his debt to the imaginative contributions of the company that first staged the piece. But at the same time, he cautions that "there should be no inopportune improvisations on stage, and ideas that arise from contact with the public should be incorporated only after careful consideration, in order not to endanger the style or the very bases of the work" (571).

In *Silencio, pollos pelones* Carballido creates some arresting and convincing individuals, in spite of the seemingly impromptu nature of the characterizations. The naiveté of the politically ambitious Eustaquio Téllez Girón (Tiquín to his aunt Leonela) is an effective foil for the gross figure of the corrupt learned counsel, the power behind the scenes. The gradual disillusionment of the charitable Doña Leonela after her installation as chief of public assistance serves as an effective contrast to the increasingly apparent idealism of the hard-nosed social worker, Berta. The poor are represented by irresponsible as well as deserving individuals. The *gringos*, especially, are entertaining, using anglicized Spanish such as "estos unos" and "que usted te quedes aquí." The ability to capture a characterization economically and perceptively, which is one of the highlights of this play, is consistently one of Carballido's most outstanding attributes.

The several story lines in *Silencio, pollos pelones* are telescoped one into another. There is a frame story (the pre- and postplay comments of the actors), an inner play (the story of the "empty coffin"), and a play-within-a-play-within-a-play (the flashback history of Doña Leonela's rise to power and disillusion). The many shifts are handled with facility and ingenuity. *Silencio, pollos pelones* is one of Carballido's most harmonious compositions; although it is specifically Mexican, it can be enjoyed in any country that knows the insane bungling of rampant bureaucracy.

VII   *Voyage into the Magic of Music*

Las cartas de Mozart is Carballido's most recent full-length play, and one of his longest.[12] Of the plays of nonconventional style, it is the second Mexican period piece. The setting is Mexico City during the 1870s.

In *Las cartas de Mozart* one notes first what may be Carballido's most persistent obsession, the desire to puncture affectation and pretense with satire and ridicule. Here Carballido satirizes an aspect of Mexican culture that still romanticizes the French intervention in the history of that country's self-determination.

The protagonist of *Las cartas de Mozart* is a girl named Margarita, the daughter of Malvina, and the niece of Renata, two sisters who long for the glamour of their recently lost empire, their handsome Max and "Carlotita." Margarita's godmother has left her a small inheritance, some three thousand pesos, and the disposition of this money is the motivation for the greatest part of the play's action. Margarita's mother and her aunt, who earn their livelihood by running a small notions shop in their home, want her to invest the money wisely—wisely, of course, meaning according to their direction. To assist them in this investment, they want Margarita to call upon the services of Marcelo, a priggish bore much older than Margarita whom they believe would make her a suitable husband, an opinion with which Marcelo heartily concurs.

In the midst of this struggle Margarita meets the Youth, a penniless young violinist who does, nevertheless, possess several original Mozart letters. In a display of unexpected independence, Margarita "invests" her fortune in the purchase of the letters, and then dedicates herself to translating them. Her mother dies of shock and chagrin; her aunt—before she learns that the fortune is dispersed—maneuvers to gain custody of Margarita (the money); Margarita feels terrible guilt following her mother's death, but the Youth leads her away from guilt and into a new life, aided always by the beauty of Mozart's music.

The play is one of Carballido's most complex. Margarita's emotions are interwoven with those of three male figures: Marcelo, the bore; the Youth; and Martín, an adolescent much smitten with her, constantly underfoot, and jealous of the attentions of the other two males. But Martín is a dreamer, and at the end of the play when he knows that Margarita is lost to him, his spirit is undiminished; he knows that his adventures still lie ahead.

Margarita's relation with Marcelo is simple: she despises him, he cherishes her; she is young and beautiful, and there is, of course, the money. This simplicity is complicated by the fact

that their ties are triangular. Margarita's aunt Renata and
Marcelo have been suitors for years, their union at first delayed
out of respect for Renata's widowhood, but more recently because of Marcelo's reluctance to seal the bargain. Renata still
worships Marcelo, but her jealousy leads her to destructive acts.
  The Youth is himself involved in a triangular relationship.
His first meeting with Margarita is motivated by his wish to
sell the Mozart letters in order to advance the career of a
beautiful young singer in the opera where he plays violin. When
this singer is offered an opportunity to go to Europe, she aban-
dons the Youth, and he quickly turns to Margarita, where, we
suppose, fate intended him from the beginning.
  The following, then, are the criss-crossing emotional lines in
Las cartas de Mozart: Margarita-Martín (a relation founded
largely in Martín's youthful imagination); Margarita-Marcelo (a
relation fired by Marcelo's desire for youthful beauty, and
money); Margarita-the Youth (the primary relation of the play);
Renata-Marcelo (the longtime suitor, the rejected aunt); The
Youth-Opera Singer (a relation that exists outside the action of
the play, but which affords motivation for what happens. Carballido often uses visual devices to symbolize the more abstract
emotional lines of the action, and in *Las cartas de Mozart*, one
such instance is a scene in which the Youth, attempting to catch
Margarita up in his fantasy, pulls out all the drawers of the
many cabinets of the small notions shop, and creates a web of
interwoven ribbons and streamers that parallel exactly the interweaving relations of the play.
  As often is true in the plays of nonconventional style, the
audience of *Las cartas de Mozart* might expect from the opening
a traditional and realistic play. Such is not the case, as evidenced
in a scene between Margarita and the Youth in Alameda Park.
Margarita, who is stricken with guilt following her mother's
death, is led there by the Youth, who says:

Then I'll take you to run through the Alameda among the streaming
trees, through mud, and you'll hear the songs and screeching of water-
soaked birds retiring to their nests; and we'll get wet, too, and then
come back and have a glass of wine and a cup of tea and you'll have
a deep, sweet sleep, and a dream that your mother is giving you
her blessing. Come on. Come! (67)

Inside the park Margarita sees only ugliness, mud, dripping trees, and shadowy figures "performing confused actions, scarcely visible; but one can intuit obscenities" (40). Then, infected by the Youth's magic, Margarita sees ordinary objects in a new way: "It is a wet rock, a round, wet rock covered with damp earth, with tiny little insects moving over it and beneath it. A rock capable of transformation and mysteries" (68). As she leaves the park, Margarita's mood has changed; she now sees fireflies and sparkling lights: "I'm not afraid any more," she tells the Youth (43).

There are other instances of nonrealistic treatment; for example, the scene in which Margarita's mother returns after death (entering *through* the wall) to recount her lonely wanderings in search of a permanent resting place. This scene is a classic example of Carballido's blending of pathos and humor.

The pervading presence in *Las cartas de Mozart* is that of Mozart himself. The Youth's entrances and exits are often accompanied by strains of his music. In the opening scene we learn that the family has just returned from a performance of *The Marriage of Figaro*. The purchase of the Mozart letters causes the death of Margarita's mother. Affected by the mood of the letters, the Youth and Margarita fantasize in several scenes, recreating the lives of Mozart and Constanza. The Youth uses Margarita's money (from the sale of the letters) to costume the young opera singer he admires for a part in *Don Giovanni*. Renata, who apparently has poisoned Marcelo in the closing scene, uses a potion she concocted from a recipe in an ancient book of poisons published in Spain but carried to Vienna, and bearing the inscription of Salieri, an Italian composer who is known to have conspired against Mozart. The dead Malvina enters to the strains of the music from the scene with the "Guest of Stone." And when the Youth comes to claim Margarita at the end of the play, she asks: "Are you Mozart now?" the Youth replies, "Almost" (91), and they leave for the premier of his opera to be performed in Vienna. In effect, Margarita agrees to play the role of Constanza to the Youth's Mozart.

Margarita leaves behind her the ghost of her dead mother, a still-daydreaming Martín, an embittered Renata, and a probably poisoned Marcelo. It is the *spirit* of Mozart, and specifically the possession of the Mozart letters and the infectiousness of the Youth's passion for Mozart's music, that saves Margarita from repeating the dreary lives of her mother and her aunt. What lies ahead is unknown, but whatever the outcome, it will be touched by the magic of Mozart's music.

CHAPTER 8

Style

I *The Mark of the Dramatist*

EMILIO Carballido is first and foremost a playwright. In addition to the fact that he has written a much more substantial body of drama than prose, it is also true that even the prose reveals the influence of the dramatist.

In a study of *El sol*, Jorge Rufinelli refers to Carballido as "a man of the theater," and suggests that the reason Carballido's novels are set in "a limited world" is that novelistically speaking he has no need of greater space in which to breathe. The theatrical "watershed," says Rufinelli, has absorbed any urge toward expansiveness. "In other words, Carballido has no need to embrace broad novelistic worlds, or to engage in the project of an extensive (totalizing) novel, since the 'world' of his fantasy is developed and completed in the *whole* of his work."[1]

Rufinelli adds that Carballido's novels "nourish the visual needs of the reader; they are novels in which plot has characteristics of the theater. These are novels that might easily be made into dramas or transferred to film."[2]

These comments are true. Carballido the dramatist dominates the world of Carballido the prose writer. The most direct comment on how this may have come about is provided by Carballido himself. Asked in an interview how he "found his vocation and came to express himself in theatrical works," Carballido answered: "I have written since I was very young. I read a lot of plays, and besides—in all modesty—it was always easier for me to write in dialogue than in the narrative form. I still have the little plays I wrote when I was nine. Strange, I simply began by writing dialogue. . . . It was easier for me than 'relating.' "[3]

How is the characteristic noticeable in Carballido's fiction? What are the marks of the dramatic writer? Carballido seems

149

to *see* the characters of his stories and novels as if they were performing on a stage. His fictions are essentially scenic in structure, and the majority of the lines are in dialogue. Even *Las visitaciones del diablo,* the most descriptive of any of his prose works, maintains the episodic structure of scenes. Carballido often employs theatrical conventions governing scene structure, using a double space between scenes occasioned by change of location, or by the introduction of new characters or the exits of characters already "on stage."

Though he knows intimately the internal motivations and reactions of his characters, Carballido is almost always the third-person creator; only rarely does he employ the first person. He remains outside, viewing his characters' actions as if watching a performance. Even in a book with the obvious autobiographical overtones of *The Sun,* the most intimate moments experienced by the young protagonist are recounted *indirectly,* through the intervention of the *watcher*:

> Later: the town down below. Looking at it like that, from up here, facedown on the jutting boulder, a person is almost nothing; all landscapes blend into one, and a person could actually *be* the landscape if he weren't chewing on bread and cheese, and if suddenly—for no reason at all—he hadn't thought of Hortensia, and . . . such an erection . . . and the view isn't important at all, quick, think about. . . .[4]

Later in the novel, when Carballido slips briefly into the first-person voice, the reader may actually overlook the moment. It is as if Carballido were uncomfortable, and wished to return as quickly as possible to the more familiar third person.

> But now *he* didn't think about her that way.
> Because this morning . . . the lessons Ricardo had given *him*
> Because of the burning desire *he'd* felt since yesterday
> Because of what happened in the movies.
> Because *I'm* not the same now. . . .
> *He* was alone and stripped bare, suddenly, there on the boulder. . . .[5]

In the theater, a gesture or an exchange of glances may explain action that takes place outside the view of the audience, may reveal changes or relationships or information pertinent to the current situation, without the need of a single line of exposition. The audience can interpret the new relationships *without* words. But the transferral of this technique to fiction may constitute an ellipsis. And from time to time these primarily "dramatic" ellipses do occur in Carballido's prose. This is not a fault *per se,* since a scene omitted may be more stimulating and revealing to the reader than the explicit scene. Nevertheless, the frequent ellipses in Carballido's fiction suggest that it is the playwright who controls the *vision.*

Adding to the effect of brevity is the use of elliptical sentences. Very often a basic grammatical element is missing, frequently a verb, creating a terse, telegraphic quality to the narrative that is paralleled in the sparse use of descriptive detail:

Adam, young, swarthy, timid, seated beside her, drooling, and the teacher at the blackboard: *rosa, rosae, rosam.*
Adam kissing her like crazy.
Adam on horseback.
Adam in the marriage license bureau, wearing a sheepskin jacket, very natural, very simple.[6]

The town below. The church sprawled there among tiny houses, with the glitter of mosaic work on the dome.[7]

A rhythmic, clear sound, accompanied by a screech . . . a rat?[8]

Splashing. The mulatto had jumped into the water and dived below the surface. Useless, totally useless.[9]

These isolated examples of Carballido's bare, stacatto style are typical of the entire body of his narrative, which is unusually concise and condensed. There are no frills in Carballido, no excess.

II *Form and Structure*

Carballido is very conscious of the demands that content exerts upon form. "Content and form," he has said, "are exact equivalents one separates for purposes of analysis, for practical reasons, but the idea that they may be separated is fallacious; it would be like separating the heart from the rest of the bodily organs."[10] The greatest experimentation is seen in the plays. His most traditional creations are his short stories, although he makes free use of such conventional forms as the frame story, the flashback, the adventure experienced on a "closed" voyage, or through a visitor from outside, or through the eyes of a child. His novels are similarly traditional in structure. *La veleta oxidada*, though narrated in Carballido's bare, unfleshed, "telegraphic" prose, adheres to the conventional chronological narrative mode. *Las visitaciones del diablo* consciously imitates the style of a nineteenth-century feuilleton, an episodic series of scenes leading, impellingly and chronologically, to the revelation of the evil spirit that causes the night visits of the devil: situation, complication, climax, resolution.

El sol, more poetic and more discursive than *Visitaciones*, shares with it the element of suspense. The structure is essentially traditional, except for the last chapter in which stream of consciousness is intermixed with overheard conversation intermixed with spasmodic, almost mystical, epiphanies. This chapter represents Carballido's greatest experimentation in delving into the subconscious of his characters.

Structurally, the novella *El norte* is Carballido's most experimental fiction; its fifteen chapters alternate between past and present—until the final chapter when they come together in a fictional present. *El norte* is Carballido's most perfectly structured narrative. It serves as an example of how form and content can be so inextricably blended that any other narrative method would be inconceivable.

In the world of Mexican theater Carballido is the greatest formal innovator since Sor Juana Inés de la Cruz. His interest in experimental form is evidenced in his first, still unpublished, drama, *Los dos mundos de Alberta*. Even then Carballido was fascinated with the possibility of portraying on stage the imaginary world that exists in a character's mind, a *tour de force* achieved with difficulty in the history of the theater. A similar effort to make visible the thought processes of a character was developed later in "El vestíbulo," "La triple porfía," and, most successfully, in "Medalla al mérito." One wishes Carballido would return to this interesting aspect of his theater, bringing to it the maturity of his many years of experience. Similar experimentation with form is found in "El espejo." Here a human personality is duplicated in a room's furnishings. When the room is stripped bare, the pretences of the room's occupant are correspondingly exposed. "El amor muerto" examines the limbo world following death and preceding the total loss of human substance (and includes what are surely among the most difficult stage directions in all of theater). "Las noticias del día" requires a set director to embody, that is, incarnate, newsstories being read on stage, a device similarly employed in the chilling "La bodega."

Each of the preceding plays relies heavily on experimentation with primarily surreal visual effects. Equally experimental are plays like *La hebra de oro* and "Yo también hablo de la rosa" which rely structurally on the combination of fantasy and strictest realism. *El día que se soltaron los leones*, too, is such a play, demonstrating what may be Carballido's most inventive use of the physical space of the stage. A lake is represented by actors running across the stage, fluttering silken blue banners. Rowboats on this "lake" are suspended from the shoulders of their oarsmen. An enormous variety of scenic effects is suggested, yet rules of strict realism coexist in this setting.

Concerning the use of stage *time*, one of Carballido's innovations is a kind of "flowing time" in which a narrator relates a series of actions that compress the passage of years into a few moments, as if a film were being rapidly unrolled *without* any distortion of the visual impression. In this technique *actors* move in normal time rhythms while *time* races at an exaggerated speed. This altered stage time is used most effectively in *El Almanaque de Juárez*, and, to a lesser degree, in "Un pequeño día de ira," and *Silencio, pollos pelones*.

Carballido is the first modern Mexican playwright (again, one must return to Sor Juana to find a similar expertise) to use music effectively in "serious" theater. He relies on the instant (nonverbal, noncerebral) communication of music in *Acapulco, los lunes, Silencio, pollos pelones, Las cartas de Mozart,* and "Yo también hablo de la rosa."

Carballido has appropriated the instant communication of myth in "Teseo" and *Medusa*. And he employs the external narrator—the nonfictional voice that intrudes upon the fiction of the play—in at least three works, *Silencio, pollos pelones*, "Un pequeño día de ira," and "Yo también hablo de la rosa." Carballido's approach to his material changes constantly; he is always seeking a more effective method of communication.

In addition, in each of these experimental approaches, Carballido is consistently aware of the appropriateness of external form. *Medusa*, the recapitulation of a classic theme, is structured in five acts. The period, or nonrealistic, pieces use the *jornada*, a form Carballido borrows from the Spanish Golden Age. Many experimental pieces have no division of time or scenic space. And as one would expect, the most traditional of his plays follow the traditional three-act structure. The form fits the content. The content dictates the form. No other Mexican dramatist has applied these universal truths so faithfully.

III *Setting*

Carballido, like most playwrights who are bound by the necessity of making stage setting explicit for the benefit of the director who will interpret his play, the actors, and the set director—even those sets in which the "set" is purposely absent—is clear and concise in delineating the settings of his plays. Much more interesting is the absence of this information in his narrative prose. Does one, again, note the mark of the creator who already *sees* the setting, and subconsciously expects his reader to see it as well? Although location is usually pertinent to the atmosphere of the prose, very little specific detail exists, especially in his earliest work, and particularly in his short stories. In the novels there is a progressive attention to physical detail, culminating in the most visual descriptive passages in *El sol*, the most recent prose work.

In the short stories the only times the reader is aware of place, or the details of a setting, occur when these details figure directly in the actions of a character. In "Las conferencias" Carballido describes the flavor, the ambiance of the town: "horses's hooves, chickens in a chicken yard, insects [notice that these are all aural cues], and the inevitably popular, casually folkloric quality. . . ."[11] The essence of the town is described, the foreignness that causes the protagonist to feel alone and isolated, but nowhere is there any physical detail of the town or architectural description of the hotel where the lecturer is staying.

In "El cubilete" the reader is aware that the action takes place in a cafe: "A boy hurriedly picked up the beers" (106), but there is not a line of physical description.

In "La caja vacía" one physical detail is essential to the story: the size of the hovel where the family of the drowned man lives. The reader is acutely aware of spatial dimensions, because the point of the story is that the room cannot accommodate the elaborate coffin sent by the well-meaning social worker. The reader, however, knows only that the coffin will not fit. Lack of space is the only physical detail; there is no description of the appearance of the room.

In other stories, too, one's impressions of dwellings, whether mean or comfortable, come from the general social condition of the family, not from description of their physical surroundings.

A partial exception is the story "Las flores blancas," in which the appearance of the guest bedroom is used symbolically. Here the flowers and their containers are carefully described, but this bedroom is the only room in the house that the reader can "see" in any detail. In "La desterrada," as well, flowers, plants, their containers, and their arrangement are described with care. But once again this description is necessary as a functional part of the story; physical detail is never used expressly to provide a sense of place.

Carballido's novels are characterized by more physical detail than his short stories, but here, too, certain interesting generalizations may be drawn: nature is usually the focus of any descriptive detail, and the tone of the language used in the description is usually poetic. For example, *La veleta oxidada* contains but three or four paragraphs that describe place. Only one of these describes the house where the major action of the novel takes place, and these few lines are devoted to an abandoned room. We have no idea what the house looks like, inside or out. Of all the *places* in the book, the one most clearly defined

for the reader is the road between the Luna home and their
mountain farm:

A pale, anemic sun seemed to be imitating the moon amid a
whirlwind of clouds. The heat was heavy, tangible. The road kept
rising through showers of water falling from the heavy branches, and
she saw that below, the palms and banana trees were swaying with
a perceptible rhythm. "Everything is the color of an eclipse," and
with anguish and sadness she rejected the many images that came
to her to describe it all. (85)

Two comments should be noted here. Though "many images"
come to Martha's mind to describe the view, they are not
developed. Even more important, the intent of the passage still
is not to describe the countryside; the function here of physical
description is that of setting a mood, of augmenting the anguish
of a character, not that of laying a scene before the reader's
eyes. One may think of the role of nature in the romantic
movement, and may wonder whether Carballido is not more
closely allied with the nineteenth than with the twentieth
century in his use of nature. In Carballido, nature sympathizes
and empathizes with the humans lashed by its forces, or lulled
by its beauties. Once again, all the components in Carballido's
writing contribute to the importance of character, the focus
on the human.

In El norte, for the first time, there are references to the
physical details of a house: "Aristeo thought about the painting
Isabel had bought for the living room: a sumptuous garden,
women wearing wigs and men fluttering with lace stepping into
flower-bedecked boats, while cupids flited about their heads"
(7); "The living room seemed luxurious, so many things, and
the huge portrait of Porfirio Díaz" (24). While describing, to a
degree, the world Isabel lives in, even more importantly, these
details contribute to her characterization.

When Isabel and Aristeo go to the seashore for their vacations, Carballido succinctly describes their boardinghouse:
"Those black and white mosaic tiles, the ferns, the rocking
chairs, the hum of the ceiling fans. It was like a warm feeling
of celebration, that feeling that floated in the quiet air of the
street and clung to the walls of this patio" (81).

Stringent as it is, this is the greatest sense of physical orientation Carballido has offered the reader to this time. The weather and the sea are basic to the concept of the novel, and there are passages throughout the book describing the fog, the beach, the sea—once again, the general atmosphere rather than the specific physical detail of the setting.

It is not coincidence that *Las visitaciones del diablo* contains still more detail. *Visitaciones* is a gothic novel, and the aura of the Estrella house is of tantamount importance to the tale. Even so, the reader has a much richer sense of atmosphere than he does of specifics. He remembers dark corridors, a rushing stream, gardens, candles, the rich *perfume* of a place—although he could not reproduce the architectural style of the house or draw a plan of the garden.

In *El sol,* Carballido's most recent novel, description is again extremely simple:

> It is a large house, with little furniture. Here in the dining room, for example, there's an enormous sideboard carved in heavy relief, crests of fruit and cedar garlands, the varnish dull and fly-specked; it contains pieces of pewter and porcelain, wooden spoons, clay cookingpots. The table is long and rough, the chairs don't match. A bare lightbulb hangs from the ceiling. . . . In the bedrooms there are cots with limp, very clean sheets, chamberpots in the bureau, when there is a bureau, if not, beneath the cot itself. (12)

Though typical of the general tone of Carballido's prose—bare, terse, simple, essential—this is certainly his most developed use of physical description. This passage *is* meant to "paint a picture." The remainder of physical description in *El sol,* the "sun" of the title—the pines, the crisp air, the lake, the cold—serves to impress the reader with the atmosphere of place, not its details.

One may see, then, that Carballido is increasingly aware of the effect and function of place in his prose fiction. Too, as the description increases the prose style correspondingly "fleshes out." The shorthand effect of *La veleta oxidada,* which in some ways resembles an outline for a work to be written later,[12] is superseded by a more conventional narrative style in the later prose works.

One might note an anomaly in the short stories of *La caja vacía*, published in 1962, four years after *El norte*, and a few years before the last two novels. There is a seeming paradox in the fact that though place is not explicitly detailed in these stories, their provincial setting is actually the unifying factor of the collection. It seems strange that they contain almost no specific physical description, but it is stranger still that they manage to convey a sense of place, a strong aura of provincial atmosphere, without the meticulous detail of many craftsmen of the short form.

In summary, these factors may to some degree be explained by the fact that basically Carballido sees the *drama* of a location. He is interested in the effect that setting has on his characters and how the mood of place contributes to their actions. He is simultaneously attracted and repelled, for instance, by the cultural lag in the provinces. He is concerned with the stultification of lives that may result from an accident of residence. At the same time, he is aware of the narcotic quality of nostalgia, aware of the fascination of immersion in an irretrievable past. He often writes about the past, or about an area where the old ways linger on. In one way, one might say that the past is a *place* in the corpus of his work.

IV   Gothic Evocations

The gothic evocations of place so important to *Las visitaciones del diablo* are equally important in many of the plays, where unseen forces generate a power that directly influences the lives of characters. Besides the broad influence of the provinces seen in much of his work, both prose and theater, Carballido often demonstrates the effect of specific locations. The provincial estate, for example, that is the setting for *La hebra de oro*, has evil emanations. It is rundown and unkempt. One of the doors of the main room is sealed, and covered with cobwebs—though it opens magically for the entrance of supernatural characters. Bluish, geometric stains mark the empty spaces where pictures have hung. In one way or other, everything connected with that property is evil, derelict, or mournful. The salvation of the land and of the people who live on the land results only after a consciously magical series of events has exorcized the malign spirits of the place.

In *El día que se soltaron los leones* Chapultepec Park evinces a specific influence on events that take place within its boundaries. In this area absurd and irrational actions seem commonplace. The stage directions make it clear that the power of *place* is intentional: "The cat must be fictitious, mysterious, never a real cat. . . . On the island the trees must create mysterious areas of intimacy. . . . The swan must be exaggeratedly poetic and delicate. . . . The lights must be exaggerated, unreal, brightly colored. . . ." (252). Inside the park all rules of behavior, all perceptions of reality, are radically altered and a new and more intense reality is created. It is not surprising that Ana, the play's heroine, elects to remain inside the zone rather than return to the conventional reality "outside."

El relojero de Córdoba, too, demonstrates Carballido's propensity for using place as an *affective* force in his theater. Don Leandro, the magistrate, at least twice discusses the feelings he has about the town of Cordoba:

DON LEANDRO: Cordoba, Cordoba, whoever had the idea of founding you, anyway?

OFFICIAL: Thirty gentlemen, sir.

DON LEANDRO: I know that. I'm one of them. But we must have done something wrong when we founded it here.[13]

OFFICIAL: That's a very strange dream.

DON LEANDRO: Yes, very strange. I don't know. The Mulatta, the Clockmaker, and now this dream. I tell you, I think we made a mistake when we founded Cordoba.[14]

The emanations from the soil to which the magistrate alludes go a long way toward explaining the strange series of events that take place in the *Relojero*.

The gothic influence of place is similarly important in a number of other plays. The setting of the rundown hotel in one of Carballido's earliest works, the unpublished "El vestíbulo," is an example. And setting is an integral part of the macabre trilogy *El lugar y la hora*, particularly in "El amor muerto" and

"La bodega," where the decay extends to the characters themselves.

In short, whether or not the result of the need to guide actors, directors, and designers, the fact is that Carballido does give more attention to setting in his plays than in his prose fiction. And, tangentially, it is clear that in these works Carballido capitalizes on the drama inherent in physical settings.

V *Characterization*

Character is the salient feature of Carballido's writing. His central preoccupations are the interrelationships among characters, the events that move characters, the crises that create change in characters, the forces that destroy them, and the epiphanies that illuminate them. In creating character Carballido is the dramatist supreme. It is the dramatist who creates his characters, even in the narrative prose. In the same way he seems to expect his reader to "see" the physical settings of his prose, Carballido seems to expect the reader to "see" the characters as if they were before him on a stage. He rarely describes his characters. And what the reader knows about a character is learned through what the *character* does and says, and what others say about him, not from information provided by the narrator. The narrator's freedom to shape and mold his characters is not invoked.

Primarily, this is the dramatist unconsciously following the rules and modes of theater within a prose fiction format, but there is one additional, more philosophically oriented factor at work, and that is that Carballido rarely judges, or even directs a judgment on the part of his reader. With few exceptions, he leaves decisions and appreciations to his reader/audience. As Emmanual Carballo has said, Carballido is a "demonstrative" rather than a "directive" writer.[15] Whatever the cause, then, the result is that Carballido's characters develop with a great deal of autonomy and a minimum of author intrusion or direction.

Once one has been introduced to Carballido's characters—his people, one is tempted to say—they are not easily forgotten. There is the family group that appears in two plays (*Un vals sin fin sobre el planeta* and *La danza que sueña la tortuga*) and the short story "Los huéspedes": Aminta and Rocío, Victor and Guillermina, and especially the young Carlos, who by extension is also the Mario Escudero of the quasi-autobiographical *El sol*. Martha Cruz Roca of *La veleta oxidada* and Isabel, Aristeo, and Max of *El norte* are startingly real considering the stringency of the narration in which they are presented. And equally memorable are Alda ("El espejo"), the Nahual and the Critic ("La zona intermedia"), Martín, the Clockmaker, and the Benito Juarez we come to know in "El Almanaque de Juárez."

It has been noted that Carballido does not often develop character through description or by *telling* the reader that the character is good or bad, happy or despairing. That is not to say he does not have a wide variety of devices through which he creates character. One technique he uses is that of removing a character from his normal orientation. The result is to create a new aspect or facet of character, altering our traditional perceptions of role and function. The angels in "La zona intermedia," for example, have great difficulty in managing the "effects" of the dawn. They are not seen as supernatural beings, but as fumbling human beings, and they are memorable. The lions in *El día que se soltaron los leones* are not predators in their confrontations with Ana, but kittens. It is easy for the audience to side with the lions rather than with their human pursuers. Again, a reversal of roles. Most illustrative of this technique is the way Carballido changes the character of Medusa and Theseus. Once removed from the cloisters of the mythology they have long inhabited, and invested with humanity—whether good or evil—they are memorably new and, unforgettably, *Carballido*'s Theseus and Medusa.

In *Te juro, Juana* comedy is used to create character. Estanfor cannot say two words without getting his tongue twisted, and he cannot perform a simple act of love without complicating it unnecessarily. Estanfor is the essence of comic ineptitude, and this general incompetence, "set" by the use of comedy, is the basic aspect of his character. In "Un pequeño día de ira" Carballido employs the now classic device of *Our Town*, the narrator who describes and comments on the actors. And in *Felicidad* Mario Ramírez Cuevas, the frustrated, embittered professor, is delineated by what people say *about* him, "Yes, it's true, he's selfish, and he's stingy" (46), as well as his own utterances; nothing that anyone says about this unpleasant character has as much effect as his own words in defining the meanness of his character.

In his short stories, Carballido usually portrays a brief segment of a life, depicts one principal action in that segment, and then develops character through the interactions and reactions resulting from that single event ("Los prodigios," "El cubilete," "Media docena de sábanas," and "La paz después del combate").

In *El sol* character is developed more slowly. Mario, the-adult-to-be, is shaped by the progression of events in the story. The reader gathers information about the youth at the same time that he learns about himself. Again, Carballido does not provide information about character. His creation provides it.

Occasionally there is no character development at all. This occurs in the work in which Carballido is more intent on message and effect than he is on the drama of character—in *Silencio, pollos, pelones,* for example; in the brief conceit "La triple porfía"; and, to a degree, in "Un pequeño día de ira." There are recognizable character types in each, but little character development. Typically, however, Carballido's work is alive with fully developed, humorous, touching, tragic, ordinary, extraordinary, unforgettable characters.

At one time, particularly at the beginning of his career, Carballido had a tendency to identify his characters through his choice of names. Rosalba, in *Rosalba y los Llaveros*, is sunny and optimistic ("rose"/"dawn," *rosa/alba*), and the Llaveros, as Eugene Skinner has pointed out, "convey the repressive attitudes of the provincial family, the ones who lock up the sexual instinct," (keepers of the keys/*llaveros*).[16] And Lázaro Llavero is a son who has been treated as an outcast for many years. Leonor is a name that Carballido gives only to sympathetic elderly characters: Leonor Luna, in *La hebra de oro*, and Leonor the grandmother in the short story "La desterrada." Luna as a family name is used in two works published a year apart, *La hebra de oro* and *La veleta oxidada*. Luna seems to have no obvious significance in *La veleta . . . ,* unless, stretching a point, it could be linked to the fanciful journey through the heavens that Martha envisions for the soul of the stillborn Luna heir, but in *La hebra de oro* Leonor Luna is a character who is most certainly not bound to earth. She is the vehicle for all the magical rituals that take place on the crumbling provincial estate. Sibila, in the same play, is an enchantress, and Mayala is the spirit of myth and dream. As Leonor is a sympathetic name, Adela is unsympathetic. Adela, sister of Adan Luna in *La veleta*, and Adela Sidel, in *La hebra*, are both narrow, unfulfilled characters. Martín is a name that may belong to innocents, for Carballido has bestowed it on the Clockmaker, and on the naive lad in *Las cartas de Mozart* who loves Margarita. Martha, in *La veleta*, carries the surname Cruz Roca ("cross"/"rock"). It is easy to assign a symbolic reading of these names to this strong but tormented person. And a possibility of symbolic interpretations is also suggested in the name of Adán, Martha's completely unsophisticated husband.

Occasionally names are used ironically to refer to qualities people do *not* possess. Nieves ("snow"), for example, in *La veleta*, is neither fair nor pure. Diogenes, in *Te juro, Juana,* claims asetheticism, but is no aesthete. Felix, in *Visitaciones*, is not happy; Angela is the opposite of angelic, and Paloma is more a tiger than a dove. Nor is Lisardo exactly a pastoral type, though the name is traditionally connected with that genre.

However, there is a tendency in some of the later works to assign simple generic names to characters: Man, Woman, Professor, Magistrate, Mayor, Narrator and Intermediary, and one assumes that Carballido may have abandoned name-symbolism as a mode of characterization.

Regardless of how he creates character—and a definitive analytical study of his characterization is still to be written—Carballido's deft touch, his unfailing eye and ear, turn his observation of character into creations that equal any in Mexican theater.

CHAPTER 9

Moods and Modes

I Realism and Fantasy

IN an interview in *La Capital* a questioner repeated a commonly held view that part of Carballido's work represents the so-called Mexican neo-realism. In response, Carballido exploded:

> As for me, I'm fed up with generic terms used in that way! . . . When I began—say in *Rosalba* or *La tortuga*—I hadn't the remotest idea of any social context; that was something that came later, perhaps with *Felicidad*. The majority of the things I do are *not* realistic; these days a minimum of my work is of that style. Many pieces have narrators, or have no set, or work through a series of expressionist or didactic or surrealist motivations. My realistic works? I guess there are about five.[1]

In spite of Carballido's heated response, it was difficult to classify Carballido's first well-known plays as anything but realistic, and most critics saw a clear division between them and his early fantastic works. Referring to *Rosalba, La danza que sueña la tortuga,* and *Felicidad,* Frank Dauster speaks of Carballido's "realistic phase."[2] Mary Vázquez Amaral goes a step further, saying that these plays are representative examples of a new *costumbrismo.*[3] Juan García Ponce writes that Carballido's theater "oscillates between an immediate and rigorous realism . . . and . . . works of imagination."[4] To the trilogy of the realistic plays, "those of everyday life," Dauster adds a second trilogy, "those of a search for being."[5] Alyce de Kuehne, in her book on contemporary Mexican theater, comments that from the beginning Carballido alternated "imaginative abstractions with neo-realism or costumbrism."[6] Willis Knapp Jones calls Carballido a

164

neo-realist, and says, though this is not actually the case, that *La danza que sueña la tortuga* "combines the two currents that characterize Carballido's work: realism and fantasy."[7] Vázquez Amaral contrasts the trilogy she calls costumbristic to "a second well-defined tendency..., the use of fantasy."[8] In the early plays this was a convenient distinction to make, and according to the critics, the lines were clearly drawn.

But following that period, Carballido's work has been much more difficult to classify, too inventive and too complex to be confined within easy generalities, and more recent writers like Joseph Vélez and Solomon Tilles agree with Carballido that the number of strictly realistic plays is limited in number. Juan Tovar, writing in *Letras de Veracruz*, denounces the "all too superficial critical commentaries that, for example, classify *Rosalba* as a 'provincial middle-class satire,' or as a 'costumbristic comedy.' "[9] Tovar's thesis is that *Rosalba* is universal in theme, more a psychological work than a satire on provincial manners. Whether or not one accepts this view completely, it is one that makes the realistic/fantastic classifications less viable.

Silencio, pollos pelones is a good example of the many plays that cannot be classified either as realistic or fantastic. On one level the play is a political satire, a scathing commentary on the ineptitudes, and the actual perversions, of corrupt government. A primary story line concerns the family of a drowned man that cannot afford to hold a wake for his memory—absolute realism. But realism in the theater has been taken to mean that everything happening on the stage could possibly be taking place in the house or apartment next door, and that if one of the walls of those dwellings were removed one could witness the same events taking place before his eyes—and in the same sequence. In these terms, *Silencio, pollos pelones* is not a realistic play, for the way Carballido presents facts and truths is far from traditional. There are no breaks between scenes. There is no chronology. Music is used as an integral part of the plot. A "chorus" enacts multiple roles and then steps outside them to address the audience directly. Thus *Pollos* is not realistic. But neither is it fantastic. It is firmly rooted in the everyday world of poverty and politics, and its characters are real people, not fictional beings. It combines formal inventiveness and real-

ism, and may best be called nonconventional, a classification
defined in the first chapter of this study. As in most of his major
plays, Carballido retained the best of traditional theater while
experimenting with form to create a style easily distinguishable
as his own. It is not surprising that Carballido rejects traditional
classifications as applied to his work.

These remarks apply equally well to his prose. The short
stories, like a *few* of the plays, are essentially realistic, but the
novels, like the majority of the plays, are not so easily classified.
Many passages are poetic in tone, verging on the impressionistic;
in *El norte*, particularly, chronology is interrupted: the *Visitaciones* adopts the external form of a nineteenth-century feuilliton
while operating on several planes of reality and interpretation;
La veleta oxidada is a sketchbook more than a complete novel.
The novels, too, can best be described as nonconventional, and
the fact that so many characteristics of drama can be seen in
Carballido's narrative prose lends credence to that classification.
What the reader/critic has learned after a number of years of
observing Carballido's writing is not to attempt to define his
creation in simplistic or definitive terms.

II   *Humor and Poetry*

Frank Dauster has said that humor and tenderness are the
two most characteristic elements in Carballido's writing.[10] Mary
Vázquez Amaral says, similarly, that "almost all of Carballido's
dramatic works contain some element of humor."[11] Humor *is* a
Carballido hallmark, but one should note that Vázquez Amaral
is referring to works of theater. And that is the limitation that
must be made: humor appears almost exclusively in Carballido's
drama. For reasons not readily apparent, the tone of Carballido's
prose is serious, and often actually somber. Contrast the treatment in prose and drama of similar situations: for example, the
sexual attraction between a young man and a considerably older
woman. *El norte*, a novella, is not a "funny" work. Yet *Te juro,
Juana*, which treats the same basic situation, has been called
"one of the most solidly, authentically, and unremittingly comic
works in recent theater."[12] Another example of different treatment of a similar situation is seen in works where a young boy

serves as the focal point. In the short story "Los prodígios" and
the novel *El sol* the worlds of these children are somber and
disillusioning. Similar children in the plays *La sinfonía doméstica*
and *La danza que sueña la tortuga* live surrounded with comedy
and gaiety—even when the problems they encounter are serious.
Carballido's prose fiction is seldom humorous, nor is all of
his theater. Examples of humorless plays are *Conversacion entre
las ruinas*, a recapitulation of destroyed lives; the surreal trilogy
El lugar y la hora; Carballido's first, and still unpublished, play,
Los dos mundos de Alberta; and the first conscious combination
of realism and fantasy, *La hebra de oro*. The reasons for the
lack of humor in these plays seems clear. Carballido himself
has commented that one does not separate "the heart from the
rest of the bodily organs."[13] The "heart" in these plays dictates
their serious treatment. Necrophilism, murder, dream, decay,
the surreal and the grotesque, are seldom humorous. Even so,
one question remains unresolved, and that is why seriousness
is the rule in Carballido's *prose*.

But to return to the original thesis, Carballido's plays abound
in humor, ranging from compassionate warmth to pure burlesque.
The many inventions of comic humor, like the infinite recourses
in characterization deserve closer examination.

One might begin with one of the oldest and most blatant forms
of humor—the kind often labeled "low." In *Te juro, Juana* humor
derives from broad farce: the lechery of Diogenes; the externally
ludicrous pairing of a schoolboy and a middle-aged woman;
and the unashamedly repetitious comic beat of Estanfor's tongue-
twisting mutilation of the language (similar to the clapping of
the slapstick from which this humor takes its name). Similarly
farcical is the French comedy atmosphere of *La sinfonía doméstica*, the in-one-door-out-the-other shuffling of wives, and the
suggestively lewd parade of prostitutes and clients. Certain
scenes from *El día que se soltaron los leones* are sheer vaudeville; billy clubs, enormously outsized shoes, the fast turns and
screeching stops of vaudeville would not be out of place in an
early silent film. And a prudish schoolmaster so worried about
maintaining the pristine white of his suit that he asks not to be
laid on the ground when he is shot is the broadest kind of humor.
Silencio, pollos pelones carries the inherently comic language

of bureaucratic reports to the realms of the wildly hilarious, a device also used in the brief play "El Censo." In each of these plays subtlety is never intended; here, too, comedy thrives on the free-swinging visual appeal to the belly-laugh conventions of burlesque. Few dramatists, certainly not Mexican dramatists, have achieved such extremes of broad comedy in plays of primarily serious intent.

Perhaps more sophisticated, but still broadly comic, is the device of humor evolving from anachronism and anomaly, the shock of the unexpected: a drunken "kiddies' Santa" in "Un cuento de Navidad"; a critic appearing in "La zona intermedia" as a "strange ... mixture of Cubist painting ... and Picasso's sculpture"; a minotaur who snivels in a corner of his labyrinth until his mother arrives bearing chicken soup and a muffler to protect him against the damp. Carballido is a master of this kind of comic invention. Probably nowhere is this humor more effective than in *Medusa,* where gorgons's claws—to their dismay—cause runs in their silk stockings; where slaves sell "filthy" French postcards in Grecian markets; where Danae, the mother of the demigod Theseus, lies in her tub yelling for a hairdryer; and where Danae's servants, wearied by almost-hourly accounts of the glorious shower of gold rained on her by Zeus, snidely speculate that at this point "she'd be damned happy to settle for a little trickle." This is perhaps the most personal of Carballido's comic modes. There is something essentially puckish about his nature, and though difficult to define with precision, this humor is probably most typically Carballido of all.

A third form of humor can be identified as that resulting from a compassionate, warm, and nostalgic affection for his characters. This is the humor of *La danza que sueña la tortuga* and *Un vals sin fin sobre el planeta.* It is the humor that cloaks Magda and Chuchis, the two shopworn ladies of "Delicioso domingo," in affectionate warmth, shielding them from ridicule. In *El relojero* this humor makes Casilda beautiful, in spite of her nearmoustache, and Martín heroic, in spite of his posturing and posing. In *Las cartas de Mozart* this humor saves Martín from being a preposterous cliché of lovesick youth, and in *Rosalba y los Llaveros* it makes us laugh affectionately, rather than cruelly, at the dotty aunt, Incarnation of the Cross. This human compassion in Carballido is described by Rosario Castellanos as *sympathy*. She has said that Carballido "has always used sympathy as a means of access to his creatures, a way of understanding them, of interpreting them...."[14]

Occasionally, nonetheless, Carballido's humor is formed from sarcasm, heavy irony, and the well-placed barb. This is the cruel humor of Mario, the frustrated professor in, ironically, *Felicidad*. This is the embittered "voice" of a prostituted and raped Acapulco seen "the morning after" in *Acapulco, los lunes*. And this is the cutting tongue of the imperfect "La perfecta casada."

The prevalance of humor in Carballido gives credence to the thesis that his world vision is essentially humorous, as opposed to those, say, whose vision is essentially tragic. This subsumes the corollary proposition that laughter is Carballido's reaction to man's helplessness before forces beyond his control. Whatever the larger philosophical reasons, the practical application is that through humor Carballido avoids pedantry, propaganda, preaching, moralizing, and just plain boredom. Carballido changed the nature of Mexican theater through the use of humor, and a Carballido without humor is inconceivable—a Strindberg without dreams, a Brecht without a social consciousness. Carballido has stamped humor with his personal mark, and humor, in turn, has served Carballido well.

Secondary in importance to the mood of humor, but still a major characteristic of Carballido's drama and prose voices, is the poetic mood. As one would expect, this voice appears most often in the nonconventional works, and often accompanies moments in which characters perceive an instant of magic (Quique, in "Los prodigios"), question the meaning of their reality (Aristeo, in the closing pages of *El norte*), or note a kind of pantheistic fusion with nature (the corn that grows magically as Leonor rocks Sibila's baby at the close of *La hebra de oro*). These poetic interludes appear in the earliest of Carballido's writing, his first play, the still unpublished *Los dos mundos de Alberta*, and continue throughout the body of his work; *El norte*, *La veleta oxidada*, "El amor muerto," *Medusa*, *El relojero de Córdoba*, *La hebra de oro*, "El espejo," "Medalla al mérito," *Las cartas de Mozart*, and *Un vals sin fin sobre el planeta*, all contain, to differing degrees, moments of poetry, but the poetic voice is most fully developed in the play "Yo también hablo de la rosa" and in the novel *El sol.*

"La rosa" is an extended metaphor concerning the nature of reality. The three reenactments of a realistic event, a train wreck, present three conflicting perceptions of reality, an individual/psychological reality, a sociological reality, and a mystical/poetical reality. These realities, in turn, are paralleled in the perceptions of the rose—the individual petal, the whole rose, and the very matter of which the rose is composed. As pointed out earlier in this study, Carballido's view is poetic, the rose seen in its essence. The Lecturer states, "There are neither petals nor roses. There is merely a web.... That fabric is basic matter, living matter . . . only a homogeneity of miraculous fictions, and one is called 'rose' and others are called by different names, one miracle after another, everywhere" (21). At the same time a second character, the Intermediary, describes the pantheistic union that had transformed the children who caused the train wreck: "The children were becoming part of everything surrounding them: they were the dump, the flowers, and they were clouds, amazement, pleasure, and they saw . . . and they understood . . . and that was all" (21).

Eugene Skinner says that this mood creates a "complex web of creative potential . . . that transcends . . . the limits imposed by analytical rationalization of human existence."[15] The identical mood is experienced by Mario, the adolescent protagonist of *El sol.* Maturing through grief, experiencing the poignancy of knowing he has emerged from a phase of his life to which he can never return, he is, for an instant, one with nature—and with knowing.

But more. Knowing is an atrocious compromise, it is accepting something that crushes and obliterates us—something I will never understand but is like radiating light, and must be known. It is something excessive, I knew it once, that dazzling harmony, that web dissolving or expanding from treetop to treetop, and this is the same but in a different way, a game and a frightening network of multiple relationships unfolding into the design of a fan that includes everything . . . and the lineal geometry of the fire being born and kindled like a thousand individual dawns on every pine needle and on

every rock and in the grains of dust and in the heart and the vital
center of the sky like a spurt of blood, of meaning . . . of panic.
"Yes. It's dawning. Yes. That's how it is. Yes, I undersand. Yes.
I can't bear it. Yes."
The sun.

This moment of "oneness," of being a part of all things, frequently occurs in Carballido's works. These moments exhibit a
tremendous sympathy and tenderness for mankind that is one
of Carballido's outstanding personal attributes, as well as one
of his most important creative moods.

III *Themes*

One cannot consider Carballido's writing without mentioning
the pervasive theme of social criticism. In this concern Carballido is squarely within the mainstream of Mexican, and, in the
broader spectrum, Spanish American, literature. Social criticism
may be implicit—the satiric sequence, say, in *Las cartas de
Mozart* in which Malvina and Renata mourn the loss of their
handsome "Max and Carlotita"—or explicit, as in his most overtly
propagandistic piece, "Un pequeño día de ira," which Osvaldo
López said offers only one solution to the Third World—violence,[16] and Dauster, "the clearest formulation of the essentially
rebellious spirit of Carballido."[17] Critics have frequently overlooked the social content of Carballido's works, and to date no
one has stated that in all of his writing there is but a handful
of works that do *not* carry some social message. Carballido, for
example, has commented that in an article comparing three of
his plays to the traditional form of the *auto sacramental,* the
"political shadings of the Lions *completely* escaped . . ." the
critic: "For me . . . the Lions are identical to the Soviets, the
tramp, to the citizens of our world, Mexico and your country.
There's nothing to do but yell at children not to be stupid,
because . . . what can you do? Tell them stories, and shout at
them. . . ."[18]

Much of Carballido's work can be classified as *essentially*
social, "Un pequeño día de ira," *El día que se soltaron los leones,
Acapulco, los lunes, El relojero de Córdoba, Silencio, pollos
pelones,* and, to a lesser degree, *Las estatuas de marfil, Felicidad,
Rosalba y los Llaveros, Te juro, Juana, Medusa,* "Yo también

hablo de la rosa," most of the plays in the collection *D.F.*, as well as several of the short stories of *La caja vacía*. Carballido's dedication to social reform, his acuteness as a social commentator, his subtlety as a social satirist, must not be overlooked. He clearly continues the traditional social concerns of two centuries of Spanish American writing.

There is a related theme, perhaps merely one aspect of the central theme of social criticism, in Carballido's treatment of the status of women. The theme of the "wasted life" emerges through examinations of customs and prejudices, but it also includes a more universal questioning of purpose and justification for life. In every context, Carballido stresses the rights of individuals, but he seems particularly insistent in his affectionate portrayals of women like the two aunts in *La danza que sueña la tortuga* and *Un vals sin fin sobre el planeta*. Aminta and Rocío, along with Leonor, in *La hebra de oro*, are women who are beginning to realize that they have lived lives with very little purpose. Now they are feeling the first stirrings of independence. Other women, Rosalba, in *Rosalba y los Llaveros*, and Ana, in *El día que se soltaron los leones*, actively rebel against their situation. Alberta, in *Los dos mundos de Alberta*, narrowly escapes being sold by her mother in return for funds to support a parasitical boy friend. Similarly, Margarita, in *Las cartas de Mozart*, thwarts the plan of her mother and aunt to sell her to a wealthy family friend—for the benefit of the mother and aunt. Juana defies the conventions of her age in her romance with a younger man. Isabel, of *El norte*, flouts contemporary sexual and societal conventions. Martha Cruz Roca, of *La veleta oxidada*, is the spirit of rebellion against provincial mores, and though ultimately she is "punished," she wins the sympathy of those who formerly had persecuted her. Paloma, in *Las visitaciones del diablo*, scorns the members of the household who considered themselves superior to her. Women of lower social class, prostitutes, "loose women" in general, receive great sympathy from Carballido: Nieves, in *La veleta oxidada*; Magda and Chuchis, in "Delicioso domingo"; the gorgons (and Medusa!) in *Medusa*; Liuba, in *Acapulco, los lunes*; Celia, in "Una rosa, con otro nombre"; and Doña Cándida, in "La fonda de las siete cabrillas." Though Carballido may criticize the society, the poverty, and the conventions that have trapped them, one must search diligently to find an unsympathetic woman character in his canon.[19] Frustrated, newly emancipated, ignorant, loved, Carballido's women are affectionately created, and this affection makes their entrapment intolerable. Carballido intently focuses a critical eye on the situation of women.

The larger, not specifically feminist, view of humanity—the definition of the individual, his rights *and* his responsibilities—is also prevalent in both Carballido's prose and drama. Man's responsibilities are the specific theme of "Teseo," for example, and that of the role of Perseus, in *Medusa*. Each of these individuals shifts the balance of rights and responsibilities prevailing in his society. By denying the dominion of the gods and assuming for themselves the privilege of directing their own actions, Theseus and Perseus assume responsibility for the results of those actions. Each kills, and each must bear that responsibility. Each becomes isolated and must live without human love. These plays easily support the existentialist label critics have sometimes applied to Carballido's theater.[20]

Other works, too, examine the same questions, notably "La zona intermedia," in which the Nahual symbolizes man's need to *act* in order to win the privileges of life, and "Yo también hablo de la rosa," in which the question of responsibility for one's acts is a central issue. Man, in *La hebra de oro*, questions the limits of man's responsibilities in the same way most of the works with young protagonists question the broader responsibilities that come with approaching maturity: Mario, in *El sol*, and Carlos in *Un vals sin fin por el planeta* and *La danza que sueña la tortuga*. At the same time, each of these latter works is the classic novel (or play, or story) of initiation,[21] and these young protagonists are among the most tenderly treated of all Carballido's characters.

While there is a possibility for many additional thematic studies (nostalgia, frustration, the recreation of the *auto sacramental*, the domestic comedy), Carballido's major themes are socially oriented: the related question of the status of women, the nature of man's rights and responsibilities, and, the last of the major themes, the provinces.

Though the setting of much of Carballido's work is Mexico

City—the collection, *D.F.*, for instance, was specifically designed
to create a "portrait" of that city—he reveals a special fondness
for the world of the provinces. Jorge Rufinelli points out that
each of Carballido's four novels takes place during a period
of "vacations," another way of saying "in the provinces": in
La veleta oxidada, Martha lives "an eternal vacation until she
'awakens' to normal life"; *El norte* takes place during a couple's
"vacation in Veracruz"; *Las visitaciones del diablo* portrays the
very essence of provincial life; and the action of *El sol* occurs
during a school break, as "Mario and his brother live the rest
of the year in the Capital." The provinces, Rufinelli continues,
"appear continuously in Carballido as a determining sign."[22]

Rufinelli is directing his remarks to Carballido's prose, but
the same may be said of his theater. Consider the plays in which
life in the provinces is an essential component of the dramatic
concept: *Rosalba y los Llaveros*, *La danza que sueña la tortuga*,
Un vals sin fin sobre el planeta, *Las estatuas de marfil*, *Te juro,
Juana*, *Conversación entre las ruinas*, *El relojero de Córdoba*,
"Silencio, pollos pelones," "Un pequeño día de ira," and a number of other one-act plays. Equally as important is the affectionately nostalgic tone the provinces usually evoke. A good
example is "La desterrada," in which an old lady virtually withdraws from life after she finds she cannot recapture the old
ways of provincial life. The same nostalgia pervades, *La danza*,
Un vals, and *El sol*. Carballido has said that the house in "La
desterrada" *is* the house he knew as a child, and the grandmother *is* his grandmother.[23] His close personal involvement
with life in the provinces accounts for the authenticity of this
major theme in Carballido's writing.

IV *Conclusions*

In his formative years Carballido came in contact with several
of Mexico's most important literary figures: the poet Carlos
Pellicer, the novelist Agustín Yáñez, and the playwright and
poet Salvador Novo. He credits these teachers with being an
important influence in his writing, along with an eclectic assortment of additional sources: his grandmother, the Bible, mythology, Grimm, the *Thousand and One Nights*, Arthur Miller,

Tennessee Williams, Jean Anouilh (in fact, all of contemporary French and German expressionist theater), and the incomparable Mexican nun, Sor Juana Inés de la Cruz.

Carballido's writing is in some ways similar to, although not necessarily influenced by, several of his friends and colleagues, Luisa Josefina Hernández, Sergio Galindo, and Sergio Magaña. Though Carballido gallantly and quite sincerely calls Luisa Josefina "the best contemporary Mexican dramatist," that honor clearly must be reserved for Carballido himself.

Carballido has changed the course of Mexican theater. In spite of his reservations about the term, Carballido contributed a number of works to the body of Mexican neo-realistic/costumbristic plays; more importantly, he has raised Mexican theater above the customarily limited level of that genre. Carballido introduced music, humor, poetry, formal innovation, and his own unique blend of realism and fantasy into the post-World War II Mexican theater. His activities as a teacher and administrator of several schools of theater (Instituto Politécnico Nacional, Bellas Artes, and the cultural program of the University of Veracruz) have influenced the course of the careers of Mexico's current generation of young dramatists.

Carballido has a true sense of theater. He has created a concept of theater that is universal and enduring. His prose fiction is significant, but Carballido is at his best when he is his most theatrical, employing all the devices that enhance the direct communication that is theater's particular province. "Teseo" and *Medusa, El relojero de Córdoba,* the trilogy *El lugar y la hora,* utilize the magic of myth. "El espejo," "Medalla al mérito," *La hebra de oro,* and "Yo también hablo de la rosa" delve inventively into levels of individual consciousness. The basically theatrical values of music, dance, and ritual are used innovatively in "Silencio, pollos pelones," *Las cartas de Mozart,* and *El día que se soltaron los leones.* The cathartic power of humor permeates his plays. Serious Mexican theater was rocked out of its conventions by the affectionate warmth, the broad burlesque, the puckish fun of Carballido's humor.

Even though his career is far from complete, a few conclusions about Carballido's work are clear. First, he has an abiding interest in philosophical and metaphysical questions. Repeatedly, he examines the extent of man's responsibilities, probes the eternal questions of the meaning of man's existence. His central concern *is* man, the human being. Character is the most important element in his creation. All other elements are manipulated to contribute to his careful examination of his creatures, their problems, their happiness, their relationships with each other. Carballido is similarly preoccupied with the individual and society. Many of his works are protests against the restraining hand of society upon man's freedom. Essentially he is a humanist, with a warm, enduring love of mankind, a writer whose best work reaches the universal while it is always, eternally, specifically Mexican.

Carballido's place in Latin American theater is well-established. He is among the half-dozen most important Latin dramatists of this century. His reputation as a prose writer is less secure, but he has made important contributions to fiction. Carballido loves to travel, and he has taught and lectured in many countries, spreading the warmth of his personality. His work has been performed throughout Latin America, on the Continent, and in many colleges and universities in the United States, exposing this major talent to ever wider audiences. Carballido's mark on literature is assured. And he continues to write; to borrow from the closing lines of one of his best plays, "Yo también hablo de la rosa," as long as he writes, one may expect to hear:

MAXIMINO: And now all of us . . .
TOÑA: . . . all of us, clasping hands . . .
POLA: . . . will hear beat . . .
TOÑA: . . . for a long, long time . . .
MAXIMINO: . . . the mystery . . .
INTERMEDIARY: . . . of our own hearts. . . .

Notes and References

Chapter One

1. For a more detailed history of Mexican theater see José Juan Arrom, *Historia del teatro hispanoamerican (época colonial)* (Mexico City: Ediciones de Andrea, 1967), and Frank Dauster, *Historia del teatro hispanoamericano (siglos XIX y XX)*, 2d ed. (Mexico City: Ediciones de Andrea, 1973). For histories of the novel see John S. Brushwood, *Mexico in its Novel, A Nation's Search for Identity* (Austin: University of Texas Press, 1966), and also his *The Spanish American Novel* (Austin: University of Texas Press, 1975).

The biographical information in this section was supplied to the author by Emilio Carballido.

Chapter Two

1. *Texto crítico*, 2, no. 3 (January–April, 1976), 93. All translations from the Spanish in this study, both of titles and content, are those of the author. Throughout, one-act plays will be indicated by quotation marks, and full-length plays by italics.

2. In a letter to the author, January 29, 1974.

3. Unpublished manuscript, p. 14.

4. *América*, 63 (June, 1950), 181–86.

5. An *auto sacramental* is a religious or allegorical play; the term is not easily translatable into English.

6. Page numbers taken from "La zona intermedia," no. 26 in *Teatro Mexicano Contemporáneo* (Mexico City: Unión nacional de autores, n.d.); *Teatro Mexicano Contemporáneo* hereafter cited as *TMC*.

7. *México en el arte*, 8 (1949); page numbers are taken from "La zona intermedia," in *TMC*.

8. *Revista de la Universidad de México*, 13, no. 4 (1958), 8–11.

9. A *sainete* is a one-act farce; there is no exact equivalent in English.

10. Published first in *América*, 61 (1949); page numbers taken from *D. F.*, 2d ed. (Veracruz: Universidad Veracruzana, 1962).

11. Included with "La zona intermedia," in *TMC*.

12. Published first by *Prometeus*, ser. 2, (December, 1951), 61–65; page numbers from *D. F.*

13. Published first in *El Nacional*, October 5, 1952, supplement; page numbers from *D. F.*

14. Published first in *La Palabra y el Hombre*, 5, no. 20 (October–December, 1961), 685–91; page numbers from *D. F.*

15. *Revista de Bellas Artes*, 14 (March–April, 1967), 4–7.

16. *D. F.*, p. 11.

17. *La Palabra y el Hombre*, 1 (January–March, 1972), 63–71; also in the *Revista de Bellas Artes*, 19 (January–February, 1975). On page 50 Carballido explains that "Una rosa" and "Delicioso domingo" were commissioned by the government, and intended for a "popular" audience. Although they are what Carballido considers to be *true* popular theater, the government paid him *not* to perform the works.

18. Published in *i. p. n.*, Journal of the Instituto Politécnico Nacional (March, 1967), unpaged.

19. *Revista de la Universidad de México*, 25, no. 6 (1971), unpaged.

20. Sent to the author by Carballido. A dittoed manuscript printed on paper bearing the yellow seal of the Universidad Nacional de México. (Published in 1972 in *Poesía en el mundo*, no. 100.) Carballido has also adapted Miguel de Cervantes's *Numancia*, but I have not seen the manuscript.

21. William Shakespeare, *The Tragedy of Othello, The Moor of Venice*. New York: Pocket Library, 1957.

22. "Por ahí viene ya / la joven a quien yo adoro."

23. Manuscript sent to the author by Carballido. The title page reads "Basado en *Don Bonifacio*, comedia de Manuel Eduardo de Gorostiza, 183./1870." Labeled in this copy "un espactáculo con música"; in *Revista de Bellas Artes*, 19 (January–February, 1975), 50–64, this is changed to "farsa con música," although the last line reads "Fin del espactáculo." The quote from Carballido is from the *Revista de Bellas Artes* edition.

24. Page numbers are taken from a later edition: no. 27 in *Textos del teatro de la Universidad de México* (Mexico City: UNAM/Dirección General de Difusión Cultural, 1972), pp. 61–95.

25. Italics mine.

26. First published in *La Palabra y el Hombre*, 12 (October–December, 1959), 625–52. Also in the 1962 edition of *D. F.*

27. A *villancico* is a Christmas poem, to be sung.

28. Page numbers from *D. F.*

29. Published in *La hebra de oro* (Mexico City: UNAM, 1957).

30. Published in *La Palabra y el Hombre*, 6, no. 24 (October–December, 1962), 651–73.

31. Page numbers taken from "Yo también hablo de la rosa," *Revista de Bellas Artes*, 6 (November–December, 1965), 5–22.

Chapter Three

1. *La caja vacía.* Mexico City: Fondo de Cultura Económica, 1962. All page numbers are from this edition.

Chapter Four

1. *La veleta oxidada* (Mexico City: Los Presentes, 1956).
2. *Texto crítico*, 2, no. 3 (January–April, 1976), 93.
3. *El norte* (Xalapa: Universidad Veracruzana, 1958).
4. *Las visitaciones del diablo: folletín romántico en XV partes* (Mexico City: Joaquín Mortíz, 1965).
5. "Chi vuol esser listo, sia; / di doman no c'e certezza."
6. *El Sol* (Mexico City: Joaquín Mortíz, 1970). Jorge Rufinelli is in agreement with this interpretation: "Actually, the sun roughly approximates a metaphor of knowing: it is the divine eye that gives light to the world, that dissipates shadows; it *allows* one to see, and *authorizes* knowing" ("*El Sol* de Carballido: novela de la iniciación," *Texto crítico*, 2, no. 3 [January–April, 1976], 78).

Chapter Five

1. Letter to the author dated February 23, 1966.
2. Frank Dauster, "El teatro de Emilio Carballido," *La Palabra y el Hombre*, 23 (July–September, 1962), 369.
3. Page numbers from *Rosalba y los Llaveros*, in *Teatro* (Mexico City: Fondo de Cultura Económica, 1960), pp. 151–247.
4. Page numbers from a playscript given the author by Carballido.
5. Letter to the author dated February 23, 1966.
6. Translation from the title page of the playscript.
7. Last page of playscript; dated 1960.
8. Page numbers from *Felicidad y Un pequeño día de ira* (Mexico City: Universidad Nacional Autónoma de México, 1972).
9. Page numbers from *La danza que sueña la tortuga*, in *Teatro mexicano del siglo XX* (Mexico City: Fondo de Cultura Económica, 1956), pp. 133–296. The title is a line from "Pequeño vals vienés," by Federico García Lorca.

Chapter Six

1. Page numbers from *Las estatuas de marfil*, no. 15 in the series *Ficción* (Xalapa: Universidad Veracruzana, 1960).
2. Page numbers from *Te juro, Juana, que tengo ganas* (Mexico City: Editorial Novaro, 1970). First published in *La Palabra y el Hombre*, 35 (July–September, 1965), 487–560.
3. Page numbers from *Acapulco, los lunes*, a playscript sent to the author by Carballido.
4. From a letter to the author dated May 21, 1969.
5. Ibid.
6. Page numbers from *Conversación entre las ruinas*, a playscript sent to the author by Carballido.
7. Page numbers from *Un vals sin fin sobre el planeta*, a playscript sent to the author by Carballido. The title is from a poem by Ramón López Velarde.

Chapter Seven

1. Playscript sent to the author by Carballido.
2. Letter to the author dated March 11, [1974].
3. Page numbers taken from *La hebra de oro* (Mexico City: Universidad Autónoma de México, 1957).
4. Letter to the author dated March 3, 1968.
5. *American Heritage Dictionary* (Boston: American Heritage Publishing Company/Houghton Mifflin, 1969).
6. Page numbers taken from *Teatro de Emilio Carballido* (Mexico City: Fondo de Cultura Económica, 1960).
7. Letter to the author dated March 13, 1970.
8. Page numbers taken from *Teatro*.
9. Robert Graves says in his annotation to the Medusa legend in *The Greek Myths* that the legend is almost surely symbolic of the Argine conquest of Libya. Medusa represents the matriachal society reigning there, and her beheading the destruction of power.
10. Page numbers taken from *Teatro*.
11. First published in 1964 in *La Palabra y el Hombre*, 31 (July–September, 1964), 509–71.
12. *Las cartas de Mozart*. *La Palabra y el Hombre*, n.s. (September, 1974), 39–91.

Chapter Eight

1. *Texto crítico*, 2, no. 3 (January–April, 1976), 68.
2. Ibid., p. 69.

3. Alfredo Vargas, "Dos horas perdidas de Emilio Carballido," *La Capital* (July 26, 1970), 71.

4. *El sol*, p. 11.

5. Ibid., pp. 39–40; italics mine.

6. *La veleta oxidada*, p. 10.

7. *El sol*, p. 30.

8. *La caja vacía*, p. 80.

9. Ibid., p. 141.

10. Marco Antonio Acosta, "Carballido," *El Nacional*, 6 (November 12, 1972), 3.

11. *La caja vacía*, p. 83.

12. Carballido agrees. In 1976 in *Texto crítico*, 2, no. 3, he says "... although I believe that *La veleta oxidada* is very deficient— one finds in the first half a kind of shorthand version of a novel broader in scope" (93). This is a point I made in my doctoral dissertation in 1966: "This usage lends a terse, telegraphic style to the narrative, contributing to the shorthand style" (169).

13. *Teatro*, p. 45.

14. Ibid., p. 65.

15. "El libro de la semana," *México en la cultura* (May 19, 1954), 2.

16. "The Theater of Emilio Carballido," in *Dramatists in Revolt, The New Latin American Theater*, ed. Leon F. Lyday and George W. Woodyard (Austin: The University of Texas Press, 1976), p. 23.

Chapter Nine

1. Interview with Alfred Vargas, p. 71.

2. *Ensayos sobre teatro hispanoamericano*, p. 143.

3. *El teatro de Emilio Carballido*, p. 35.

4. "Las posibilidades del teatro en México: Emilio Carballido." *México en la Cultura* (November 9, 1958), p. 2.

5. *Ensayos*, p. 160.

6. *Teatro mexicano contemporáneo, 1940–1962* (Mexico City: DeKuehne, 1962), p. 111.

7. *Behind Spanish American Footlights* (Austin: University of Texas, 1966).

8. *El teatro*, p. 55.

9. "Presentación," 1, no. 1 (1973), 5–15, p. 5.

10. *Ensayos*, p. 181.

11. *El teatro*, p. 24.

12. Tovar, p. 14.

13. Interview with Marco Antonio Acosta, p. 3.

14. *Juicios sumarios* (Xalapa: Universidad Veracruzana, 1966), p. 45.

15. *Dramatists in Revolt*, p. 35.

16. *"Un pequeño día de ira*, Crítica a la realidad social en su conjunto," *Latin American Theatre Review*, 9, no. 1 (Fall, 1975), 35.

17. *Ensayos*, p. 170.

18. Letter to author dated March 13, 1970. In fairness, it should be noted that political interpretation was not the focus of the commentator's analysis, but it is significant that Carballido feels strongly enough about the social message of the play that he was compelled to comment on the critic's omission.

19. Adela, in *La hebra de oro*, is an example, Renata and Malvina, in *Las cartas de Mozart*, and the aunt, in *El día que se soltaron los leones*. It is interesting to note, however, that each is unsympathetic for a purely functional reason, that is, that they must for reasons of dramatic tension and motivation oppose the actions of the protagonist.

20. Tamara Holzapel refers to *Medusa* when she speaks of an existential vein, comparing the play to Sartre's *Les Mouches* ("A Mexican Medusa," *Modern Drama*, 12, no. 3 [December, 1969], 235). However, other critics have used the term when it is not so clearly applicable: Eugene Skinner, "Carballido: Temática y forma en tres autos," *Latin American Theatre Review*, 31, no. 1 (Fall, 1969), 37; Solomon H. Tilles, "La importancia de 'la palabra' en *Rosalba y los Llaveros*," *Latin American Theatre Review*, 8, no. 2 (Spring, 1975), 40; and Joseph F. Vélez, "Tres aspectos de *El relojero de Córdoba* de Emilio Carballido," *Explicación de Textos Literarios*, 1–2 (1973), 159.

21. Dauster would add Medusa to this list, saying that "Carballido uses this structure [that of Greek myth] to construct what we could call the arrival at a spiritual majority, what the anthropologists refer to as the 'rite of passage'" (*Ensayos*, p. 161).

22. *Texto crítico*, p. 72.

23. In a conversation with the author in Mexico, winter, 1974.

Selected Bibliography

PRIMARY SOURCES

1. Bibliography

PEDEN, MARGARET SAYERS. "Emilio Carballido, Curriculum Operum." *Texto crítico*, 2, no. 3 (January–April, 1976), 94–112.

2. Drama

Acapulco, los lunes. In Colección "Poesía en el Mundo." Monterrey: Ed. Sierra Madre, 1969.

"Almanaque de Juárez." In Colección "Poesía en el Mundo." Monterrey: Ed. Sierra Madre, 1972.

Las cartas de Mozart. In *La Palabra y el Hombre*, extra no. (September, 1974), 39–81.

La danza que sueña la tortuga. In *Teatro mexicano del siglo XX*, vol. 3. Mexico City: Fondo de Cultura Económica, 1956.

El día que se soltaron los leones. In *Teatro de Emilio Carballido*. D.F. 2d ed. Xalapa: Universidad Veracruzana, 1962.

Las estatuas de marfil. Colección Ficción, no. 15. Xalapa: Universidad Veracruzana, 1960.

Felicidad. Textos del Teatro de la Universidad de México, no. 27. Mexico City: UNAM, 1972.

"La fonda de las siete cabrillas." *Revista de Bellas Artes*, 19 (January–February, 1975), 50–64.

La hebra de oro. Mexico City: UNAM, 1957.

El lugar y la hora. In *La hebra de oro*.

Medusa. In *Teatro de Emilio Carballido*.

"Un pequeño día de ira." *Textos del Teatro de la Universidad de México*, no. 27. Mexico City: UNAM, 1972.

El relojero de Córdoba. In *Teatro de Emilio Carballido*.

Rosalba y los Llaveros. In *Teatro de Emilio Carballido*.

Silencio, pollos pelones, ya les van a echar su maíz. In *La Palabra y el Hombre*, 31 (July–September, 1964), 509–71.

Teatro de Emilio Carballido. Mexico City: Fondo de Cultura Económica, 1960.

Te juro, Juana, que tengo ganas. Mexico City: Editorial Novaro, 1970.

"Teseo." *La Palabra y el Hombre*, 6, no. 24 (October–December, 1962), 651–763.
"Yo también hablo de la rosa." In *Te juro, Juana*. Mexico City: Editorial Novaro, 1970.
"La zona intermedia." *Teatro mexicano contemporáneo*, no. 26. Mexico City: Unión nacional de autores, n.d.

3. Prose

La caja vacía. Mexico City: Fondo de Cultura Económica, 1962.
El norte. Xalapa: Universidad Veracruzana, 1958.
El sol. Mexico City: Joaquín Mortíz, 1970.
La veleta oxidada. Mexico City: Los presentes, 1956.
Las visitaciones del diablo. Mexico City: Joaquín Mortíz, 1965.

4. Translations

The Clockmaker from Cordoba. In *The Golden Thread and Other Plays,* edited and translated by Margaret Sayers Peden, pp. 151–210. Austin: University of Texas Press, 1971.
Conversation Among the Ruins. Translated by Myra Gann de Portilla. Produced but not published.
The Day They Let the Lions Loose. In *Voices of Change in the Spanish American Theatre*, edited and translated by William I. Oliver, pp. 1–46. Austin: University of Texas Press, 1971.
"Dead Love." In *The Golden Thread*, pp. 11–21.
"Et moi aussi, je parle de la rose." Translated by Xavier Pomeret. Produced but not published.
"I fiore bianchi." In *Le più belle novelle de tutti i paesi*. Milan, 1966.
"Der friede nacht dem Kampt." In *Mexiko, Llano Grande*. Stuttgart: Horst Erdman Verlag, 1962.
"The Glacier." In *The Golden Thread*, pp. 22–33.
"The Golden Thread." In *The Golden Thread*, pp. 49–119.
"The Intermediate Zone." In *The Golden Thread*, pp. 121–50.
"I Too Speak of the Rose." Translated by William I. Oliver. *Drama & Theatre*, 8, no. 1 (October, 1969), 47–60. Also in *The Modern Stage in Latin America*.
"I Also Speak of the Rose." Translated by Myrna Winer. Produced but not published.
Medusa. Translated by Mary Vázquez de Amaral. Unpublished. Manuscript in the Pan American Society of New England.
"The Mirror." In *The Golden Thread*, pp. 1–8.

The Norther. Translated by Margaret Sayers Peden. Austin: University of Texas Press, 1968.

"Die Parasiten." Produced but not published.

"A Short Day's Anger." Translated by Margaret Sayers Peden. Produced but not published.

"Theseus." In *The Golden Thread,* pp. 211–37.

"The Wine Cellar." In *The Golden Thread,* pp. 34–48.

The Sun. Translated by Margaret Sayers Peden. In manuscript.

SECONDARY SOURCES

ACOSTA, MARCO ANTONIO. "Charla con Emilio Carballido." *El Nacional* (Mexico City), November 12, 1972, p. 3. Question and answer interview focusing on broad questions concerning the profession of writing and the state of literature.

BRAVO-ELIZONDO, PEDRO. *Teatro hispanoamericano de crítica social.* Madrid: Playor, 1975. Chapter devoted to "Un pequeño día ira" [Bravo Elizondo calls it "Una tarde de ira"], chosen as most representative of Carballido's socially oriented works, in accord with Bravo-Elizondo's objective of presenting a "panorama of the theater of social criticism."

CARBALLO, EMMANUEL. "El libro de la semana." *Mexico en la Cultura,* May 19, 1957, p. 2. A review of *D.F.* Carballo notes that Carballido essays news techniques and styles in this collection, "another success for Emilio Carballido."

CASTELLANOS, ROSARIO. *Juicios sumarios.* Xalapa: Universidad Veracruzana, 1966. A chapter on Carballido presents a very general survey of his theater to 1966. Castellanos emphasizes the playwright's ability to portray man with ever-increasing comprehension and sensitivity.

————. "Obras de Emilio Carballido." *México en la Cultura,* May 15, 1960, p. 4. See chapter in *Juicios sumarios.*

CORTÉS CAMARILLO, FÉLIX. "Carballido: Si compro pan, se me acaba. Si compro dulce se me acaba. Si hago un homenaje. . . ." *Siempre,* no. 1170 (November 26, 1975), xvi. A review of *Las cartas de Mozart.* Cortés notes that the play resembles Carballido's early theater except for the more open treatment of elements of the plot which previously would have been subdued.

————. "Silencio, teatros vacíos, ya les van a dar su público." *Siempre,* no. 1040 (May 30, 1973), xvi. A review of "¡Silencio, pollos pelones, ya les van a echar su maíz!" The critic thinks that Carballido's attempts to employ humor in the play are restricted by the work's difficult, three-plot structure.

—————. "El Teatro: *Acapulco los lunes.*" *La Capital* (Mexico City), August 2, 1970, pp. 73–74. This critic believes that *Acapulco* is one of the less successful ventures of Carballido, whom he nevertheless praises in general.

DAUSTER, FRANK. *Ensayos sobre teatro hispanoamericano.* Mexico City: SepSetentas, Secretaría de Educación Pública, 1975. A long chapter devoted to the career of Carballido. Dauster, dean of Latin American theater critics, cites technical imagination and a profound humanity as being most characteristic in Carballido's theater.

—————. "El teatro de Emilio Carballido." *La Palabra y el Hombre,* no. 23 (1962), 369–84. An early general survey covering the period 1957–1962. Dauster believes that Carballido's principal contributions are his resolute experimentation with forms and his constantly deepening understanding of humanity. (See chapter in *Ensayos,* updated from time of this article.)

DEKUEHNE, ALYCE. *Teatro mexicano contemporáneo, 1940–1962.* Mexico City: de Kuehne, 1962. Pp. 109–22. DeKuehne studies Carballido's theater under two groupings: "abstract theater," and "realistic or costumbristic theater." She calls Carballido the most praised of contemporary Mexican dramatists, as well as the most consistently successful.

"La figura de la semana: Emilio Carballido." *El Heraldo de México,* January 7, 1968, supplement, p. 2. A homage to Carballido on the occasion of this newspaper's recognition of his *Te juro, Juana, que tengo ganas* as the best play of 1967. Praise of Carballido's successful integration of the comic and the profound.

GARCÍA PONCE, JUAN. "Las posibilidades del teatro en México: Emilio Carballido." *México en la Cultura,* November 9, 1958. García Ponce says that Carballido is not a didactic writer: he exposes situations, leaving conclusions to the spectator or reader.

GLANTZ, MARGO. "Todos hablamos de la rosa." *Siempre,* no. 680 (July 6, 1966), viii. Glantz comments on the unusual combination of journalistic techniques and poetic symbolism with "soft" satire and social protest in the work.

JONES, WILLIS KNAPP. *Behind Spanish American Footlights.* Austin: University of Texas Press, 1966. Pp. 408–9. Brief note. Jones calls Carballido "one of the most interesting of modern Mexican dramatists, a man who refuses to be classified."

HERNÁNDEZ, LUISA JOSEFINA. "*D.F.*" *La Palbara y el Hombre,* no. 2 (1957), 101–2. A favorable review of Carballido's collection of short theater works. Concise comments on his techniques in realistic and fantasy pieces.

————. "Homenaje." *Letras de Veracruz*, 1, no. 1 (1973), 17–23. Personal recollections of Luisa Josefina's long friendship with Carballido. Interesting and illuminating anecdotes.

HOLZAPEL, TAMARA. "A Mexican Medusa." *Modern Drama*, 12 (1969), 213–37. A general study with some specific comments on the political and philosophical implications. Holzapel compares Medusa to Sartre's *Les mouches*.

LEAL, RINE R. "Notas sueltas sobre el teatro de Emilio Carballido." *Casa de las Américas*, 5, no. 30 (1965), 96–99. A concise and informative article reflecting a Cuban point of view.

LÓPEZ, OSWOLDO A. "Crítica de la realidad social mexicana en obras representativas de Emilio Carballido." Ph.D. dissertation, University of Pennsylvania, 1973. Examines *El día que se soltaron los leones*, "Un pequeño día de ira," "¡Silencio, pollos pelones . . !", and *Almanaque de Juárez*.

————. "*Un pequeño día de ira*: Crítica de la realidad social en su conjunto." *Latin American Theatre Review*, 9 (Fall, 1975), 29–35. López stresses the political implications of the play.

MADIRACA, MARY. "La Medusa de Emilio Carballido." *Letras de Veracruz*, 1, no. 1 (1973), 25–34. See Mary Vázquez Amaral. This article is a chapter in *El teatro de Emilio Carballido*.

MONTERDE, FRANCISCO. "*La hebra de oro* y otras evasiones." *Revista de la Universidad de México*, 10 (June, 1956), 27–28. A brief commentary on the use of fantasy in contemporary theater. Carballido's play is noted as a successful example.

MURÚA, RITA. "Una visión fragmentaria de la provincia mexicana." *Revista mexicana de literatura*, 11–12 (November–December, 1962), 78–80. Review of *La caja vacía*. Murúa comments on the lack of character development and the stark portrayal of reality in this collection. She blames Carballido's use of dramatic technique for hampering his narrative style. The story "La caja vacía," however, is acclaimed for its successful development.

PEDEN, MARGARET S. "Emilio Carballido, curriculum operum." *Texto Crítico*, 2, no. 3 (1976), 94–112. Revision of bibliography published in *Latin American Theatre Review*, 1 (Fall, 1967), 38–49.

————. "Tres novelas de Carballido." *La Palabra y el Hombre*, 43 (1967), 563–79. Study of Carballido's first three novels, concluding that Carballido's primary concern is what makes and breaks human relationships. Depth of characterization is therefore more important than accumulation of events.

————. "Theory and Practice in Artaud and Carballido." *Modern Drama*, 11 (1968), 132–42. Examines Carballido in the light of Antonin Artaud's theory that "everything that occupies the stage" should be addressed "first of all to the senses . . . rather to the mind, as is the language of words." Examples cited are *La hebra de oro* and the trilogy *El lugar y la hora*.

PETERSON, KAREN. "Existential Irony in Three Carballido Plays." *Latin American Theatre Review*, 10, no. 2 (Spring, 1977), 29–35. Plays included, *Medusa*, "Teseo," and *Las estatuas de marfil*, which the author considers a trilogy: "three variations on a single theme" incorporating the existential irony characteristic of Sartre's drama.

RUFINELLI, JORGE. "*El sol* de Carballido: novela de la iniciación." *Texto crítico*, 2, no. 3 (January–April, 1976), 68–93. An excellent study by the editor of *Texto crítico*. Primary emphasis on *El sol*, but includes discussion of all novels. The thesis is that these prose works are essentially dramatic and might easily be adapted to the stage or film.

RUIZ REGALADO, MARGARITA. "El comienzo de la ira." *Conjunto*, no. 15 (1973), 59–60. A brief commentary on *Un pequeño día de ira*. The author does not consider it to be typical of the genre of political theater.

SKINNER, EUGENE R. "Carballido: Temática y forma en tres autos." *Latin American Theater Review*, 3 (Fall, 1969), 37–47. A valuable study of the "Autosacramental de la zona intermedia," *La hebra de oro*, and *El día que se soltaron los leones*.

————. "The Theater of Emilio Carballido: Spinning a Web." *Dramatists in Revolt: The New Latin American Theater*, edited by Leon F. Lyday and George W. Woodyard. Austin: University of Texas Press, 1976. Study of "La zona intermedia," *Rosalba*, *La hebra de oro*, and "La rosa." Through the progression of these plays Skinner believes that Carballido has "enriched the allegorical image of man" he first experienced in "La zona intermedia."

SOLÓRZANO, CARLOS. "El teatro de la posguerra en México." *Hispania*, 47 (May, 1964), 693–97. A general study. Solórzano places Carballido at the forefront of the *costumbrista* movement in the early postwar years.

TILLES, SOLOMON H. "La importancia de 'la palabra' en *Rosalba y los Llaveros*." *Latin American Theatre Review*, 8 (Spring, 1975), 39–44. Tilles' thesis is that dramatic tension in the work results from the psychological tactics of Rosalba and not from a collision between two conflicting classes or social traditions.

TOVAR, JUAN. "Presentación." *Letras de Veracruz*, 1, no. 1 (1973), 5–15. A general presentation of the body of Carballido's work, praising its abundance and richness, and lamenting the fact that very little has been written on it in Mexico.

VARGAS, ALFREDO. "Dos horas perdidas de Emilio Carballido." *La Capital* (Mexico City), July 26, 1970, pp. 71–80. A long interview with Carballido ranging from art and politics to past influences. Interesting and informational.

VÁZQUEZ AMARAL, MARY. *El teatro de Emilio Carballido* (*1950–1965*). Mexico City: B. Costa-Amic, 1974. Ph.D. dissertation, Rutgers University, 1970. Major study covering Carballido's theater from 1950–1965. Some grouping by style, "mitos,' "fantasía," "alegoría," and some individual essays [i.e., *Las estatuas de marfil*]. Most important work to date devoted to Carballido.

————. "*Yo también hablo de la rosa* de Emilio Carballido: Un estudio crítico." *Revista de la Universidad de México*, 27 (January, 1973), 25–29. A comprehensive study emphasizing Carballido's complex view of man. (Chapter in *Teatro*.)

VÉLEZ, JOSEPH F. "Una entrevista con Emilio Carballido." *Latin American Theater Review*, 7 (Fall, 1973), 17–24. Comments by Carballido on his work and on the theater in general.

————. "Tres aspectos de *El relojero de Córdoba* de Emilio Carballido." *Explicación de Textos Literarios*, 1–2 (1973), 151–59. An informative study, mainly concerned with the psychological aspects of the play. Discussion of humor in the work and of the evidence of literary influences manifested in it.

Index